"How grateful I am to God for Nancy G[...] study, *Saints and Scoundrels in the Sto[...]* put in the hands of all my women frie[...] [...] yet believer to the seasoned saint. Unfolding like a drama, this book presents in clear light the people with whom Jesus lived and interacted (mostly) during his earthly ministry. Like a mirror, this book beckons the reader to behold herself in the reflected light of how real people interacted with the real and the resurrected Jesus. The exposure from this reflection would be awful if Nancy was not such a faithful guide, reminding us at every turn that repentance is the way forward and that what humbles you can never hurt you. *Saints and Scoundrels* is convicting and comforting at once, reminding all true believers that God's family is rough around the edges and held together by grace and blood and faith and the King of kings and Lord of lords who makes himself lowly and gentle for the salvation of his people. The clarion call of the gospel life rings loud and true in this book. Oh, what a Savior! Oh, what a book!"

> **Rosaria Butterfield,** Former Professor of English, Syracuse University; author, *The Gospel Comes with a House Key*

"I have a deep appreciation for Nancy Guthrie's ability to commend the wonders of grace with such wonderful prose, and this book is no exception. *Saints and Scoundrels in the Story of Jesus* is a brilliant 'rogues' gallery' of redemption with a heart-stirring focus on the Saint who came unabashedly for scoundrels like you and me. Read and be refreshed again in the gospel."

> **Jared C. Wilson,** Assistant Professor of Pastoral Ministry, Spurgeon College; Author in Residence, Midwestern Baptist Theological Seminary; author, *The Imperfect Disciple*

"If you have ever felt that the Bible belongs to another world, you must read this book. Nancy Guthrie's compelling cameos will draw you into the lives of people whose interactions with Jesus are surprisingly like our own. These characters will speak directly to the realities of your life, giving you a fresh glimpse of all that can be yours in Jesus Christ. Get ready to see yourself in the scoundrels and, by God's grace, become more like the saints."

> **Colin S. Smith,** Senior Pastor, The Orchard, Arlington Heights, Illinois; author, *Heaven, How I Got Here* and *Heaven, So Near—So Far*

"Nancy Guthrie rightly sees Christ in all of Scripture. Even in the details of biblical accounts, *Saints and Scoundrels in the Story of Jesus* points to the overarching story of the one who transforms sinners. Gather some friends and get drawn into the stories to see the impact Jesus had on the lives of hypocrites, crooks, and criminals. You might just find yourself mirrored in the characters, and your heart will be stirred as you come to know Christ better."

Keri Folmar, Director of Women's Ministries, United Christian Church of Dubai; author, *The Good Portion: Scripture*

Saints and Scoundrels
in the Story of Jesus

TRUTHFORLIFE®

THE BIBLE-TEACHING MINISTRY OF **ALISTAIR BEGG**

The mission of Truth For Life is to teach the Bible with clarity and relevance so that unbelievers will be converted, believers will be established, and local churches will be strengthened.

Daily Program

Each day, Truth For Life distributes the Bible teaching of Alistair Begg across the U.S. and in several locations outside of the U.S. through 1,800 radio outlets. To find a radio station near you, visit **truthforlife. org/stationfinder**.

Free Teaching

The daily program, and Truth For Life's entire teaching archive of over 2,000 Bible-teaching messages, can be accessed for free online and through Truth For Life's full-feature mobile app. Download the free mobile app at **truthforlife.org/app** and listen free online at **truthforlife.org**.

At-Cost Resources

Books and full-length teaching from Alistair Begg on CD, DVD, and USB are available for purchase at cost, with no markup. Visit **truthforlife.org/store**.

Where to Begin?

If you're new to Truth For Life and would like to know where to begin listening and learning, find starting point suggestions at **truthforlife. org/firststep**. For a full list of ways to connect with Truth For Life, visit **truthforlife.org/subscribe**.

Contact Truth For Life

P.O. Box 398000 Cleveland, Ohio 44139

phone 1 (888) 588-7884   **email** letters@truthforlife.org

/truthforlife   @truthforlife   truthforlife.org

Saints and Scoundrels in the Story of Jesus

NANCY GUTHRIE

CROSSWAY®

WHEATON, ILLINOIS

Library of Congress Cataloging-in-Publication Data

Names: Guthrie, Nancy, author.
Title: Saints and scoundrels in the story of Jesus / Nancy Guthrie.
Description: Wheaton: Crossway, 2020. | Includes bibliographical references and index.
Identifiers: LCCN 2019025866 (print) | LCCN 2019025867 (ebook) | ISBN 9781433566097 (trade paperback) | ISBN 9781433566103 (pdf) | ISBN 9781433566110 (mobi) | ISBN 9781433566127 (epub)
Subjects: LCSH: Jesus Christ–Friends and associates.
Classification: LCC BS2430 .G88 2019 (print) | LCC BS2430 (ebook) | DDC 232.9–dc23
LC record available at https://lccn.loc.gov/2019025866
LC ebook record available at https://lccn.loc.gov/2019025867

Crossway is a publishing ministry of Good News Publishers.

BP		33	32	31	30	29	28	27	26	25	24	23	22
13	12	11	10	9	8	7	6	5	4	3	2	1	

This book is affectionately dedicated to the women of Cornerstone Presbyterian Church in Franklin, Tennessee. Some Sundays I look around the room, and I'm moved to tears by the great gift I've been given of godly women to walk with through this life of faith. Each week we come together to confess our scoundrel ways and are assured of forgiveness. We partake of a feast of God's word and the feast of the bread and the cup, and we head out into the world as "those sanctified in Christ Jesus, called to be saints together with all those who in every place call upon the name of our Lord Jesus Christ" (1 Cor. 1:2).

CONTENTS

INTRODUCTION

The story of Jesus includes all kinds of characters—a second cousin who recognized him, parents who loved him, disciples who misunderstood him, fastidious law-keepers who tried to trap him, a friend who betrayed him, priests who plotted against him, and followers who died for him. While some embraced him, others hated him. While some wanted to serve him, others wanted to use him. Some who claimed to be saints proved to be scoundrels. And some who began as scoundrels were transformed into saints.

For some of us, many of these characters are still stuck on a Sunday school felt board. We formed our understanding of who they were and the part they played in the story of Jesus long ago, perhaps in childhood, and have never come to see them in a fuller light, as more complex human beings. Others of us don't have a childhood background of Sunday school stories that have shaped our understanding of these various characters. We're more of a blank slate. Or, if not completely blank, perhaps we have some significant gaps. We're still trying to make sense of the story of Jesus in terms of why he came, what his message was and is, why he was loved by some and hated by others, and why he remains such a polarizing figure even today.

I hope to add to, deepen, refine, or perhaps correct your grasp of the various people I feature in the following chapters. I hope to show them to you from an angle you may not have seen before or at least to show them through a more intense lens than you may have previously examined them. I hope you'll come to see them in a fuller dimension in terms of their human frailty and limitations as well as their confidence and courage. I hope to show you some of the things that may have shaped their expectations, motivations, and misunderstandings. I hope you'll see some of yourself in them, at times. But mostly, I want to help you to see Jesus more clearly through delving into these stories and these people. Over and over again, we'll see how Jesus interacted with people—people with hopes, dreams, hurts, and disappointments. We'll hear what Jesus said to those who welcomed him and wanted him, as well as to those who rejected him and ridiculed him. We'll also get a sense of what Jesus wants from us and what he offers to us.

All this will take us deep into our Bibles, especially into the four Gospels—Matthew, Mark, Luke, and John—as well as into the book of Acts, as the story of Jesus continues even after his death and resurrection. To give you a solid foundation for getting the most out of each chapter, you may want to spend some time reading the Bible passages each chapter is based on before you read the chapter. To help you with this, I've created a Personal Bible Study to go along with this book that you can do on your own or work through with a group. You'll find it, along with other resources connected to this book, at www.nancyguthrie.com.

It was my own curiosity about some of these characters, my own questions about why they did the things they did and said the things they said—and for some, died the way they died—that made me want to explore their stories. Again and again, I've seen pieces of myself in them—my fears, my failures, and my desires. But more importantly, they've helped me to love and admire Christ more, to become more convinced of his goodness, and to live more fully anticipating all he has promised to share with those who take hold of him by faith. I'm praying that the study of these characters will do the same for you—that these saints and scoundrels will point you clearly and convincingly to the only hope for saints and scoundrels: Jesus Christ.

1

THE VOICE

Recently, people all over the world stopped whatever they were doing to watch something happening on the outskirts of London—the wedding of Prince Harry and Meghan Markle. As they tuned in to the ceremony at St. George's Chapel in Windsor, they heard the words of a preacher. Here's a snippet of what that preacher had to say:

> Someone once said that Jesus began the most revolutionary movement in human history. A movement grounded in the unconditional love of God for the world, and a movement mandating people to live that love, and in so doing to change not only their lives but the very life of the world itself. We must discover love—the redemptive power of love. And when we do that, we will make of this old world, a new world.[1]

Rev. Michael Curry was convinced that what the world needs is love and that love has the power to change the world. And a roar of approval for his message rose up all over the world. Curry's sermon amassed forty thousand tweets per minute, many praising the reverend's address as the standout moment from the ceremony for its style and substance.

When we begin reading at the beginning of Matthew's Gospel, we hear another kind of preacher preach: "The voice of one crying in the wilderness: 'Prepare the way of the Lord; make his paths straight'" (Matt. 3:3). This was the preacher everyone was talking about back in his day. He was the one people traveled from their homes and cities to hear, which was surprising when you consider his message. Matthew 3:2 summarizes the content of this preacher's message this way: "Repent, for the kingdom of heaven is at hand." At the heart of this preacher's message to the people of his day was that they were wrong and had to change. There had to be a radical reordering of their lives. Why? Because the King was coming. This preacher called the most religious people in town a "brood of vipers," warning them, "Even now the axe is laid to the root of the trees. Every tree therefore that does not bear good fruit is cut down and thrown into the fire" (Matt. 3:10). *Well, that's not very nice!* He warned: "His winnowing fork is in his hand, and he will clear his threshing floor and gather his wheat into the barn, but the chaff he will burn with unquenchable fire" (Matt. 3:12). *Well, that would be unpleasant!*

I don't think those guests at the recent royal wedding would have appreciated this preacher's message nearly as much as they did Michael Curry's message, do you? This preacher, whom we know as John the Baptist, was convinced that what the world needs is repentance—a turning from self and sin toward God and grace.

But let's be honest. This idea that we need to repent because judgment is coming reminds us of the cartoons we've seen with a guy on a street corner in a robe and long beard carrying a sign that says, "Repent, the end is near!" It strikes us as unnecessarily alarmist and rather ridiculous. So many of us have settled comfortably into a status quo lifestyle that would be incredibly inconvenient to disrupt. This is why it is so hard for us to significantly change our diets, for example. The suggestion that we go from enjoying our French toast and french fries and fried rice and start the Keto diet makes our stomachs growl. To give up our old device and adjust to the latest technology sometimes makes us want to hold on to the familiar version a little longer. To make a significant change in the way we interact with our boss, our coworkers, our customers, our in-laws, or our neighbors can seem like a whole lot more effort than we want to expend.

So let's look at the man, John the Baptist, and his challenging call away from the status quo, his call to everyone within the sound of his voice to turn around and go another direction from the way their whole lives have been heading. Let's look at his mission, his message, and the misunderstanding he had about Jesus. As we trace his story through the Gospels, we'll witness many who responded to his call to repentance. We'll see many who rejected his call and sought to silence him. We'll also meet a man and his wife (two scoundrels) who finally succeeded in silencing "the voice."

John's Mission

To understand John the Baptist and his mission, we simply can't begin with his miraculous conception. We have to understand that for centuries, the people of God had been watching and waiting for someone who would announce the coming of the promised Messiah. For centuries, when the scrolls of Isaiah were opened, God's people would work their way through the first thirty-nine chapters of promised judgment and then turn a corner at chapter 40 to hear:

> Comfort, comfort my people, says your God.
> Speak tenderly to Jerusalem,
>   and cry to her
> that her warfare is ended,
>   that her iniquity is pardoned,
> that she has received from the LORD's hand
>   double for all her sins.

A voice cries:
"In the wilderness prepare the way of the LORD;
  make straight in the desert a highway for our God.
Every valley shall be lifted up,
  and every mountain and hill be made low;
the uneven ground shall become level,
  and the rough places a plain.
And the glory of the LORD shall be revealed,
  and all flesh shall see it together,
  for the mouth of the LORD has spoken." (Isa. 40:1–5)

Ah, when were things going to change? When would the glory of God be revealed in what seemed to them to be a God-forsaken land? When a voice would begin crying out, calling God's people to prepare for the coming of the divine King.

Isaiah's words draw upon the imagery of a king coming to a city. A bevy of workers would go out before the king to make sure the roads were passable for him and that the people were prepared to celebrate his arrival.

It wasn't just the prophet Isaiah who wrote about this voice. Years later, God spoke through the prophet Malachi, saying, "Behold, I send my messenger, and he will prepare the way before me. And the Lord whom you seek will suddenly come to his temple; and the messenger of the covenant in whom you delight, behold, he is coming, says the LORD of hosts" (Mal. 3:1). But as the book of Malachi continues, the experience of the coming of this King to his people, this Lord to his temple, doesn't exactly sound warm and fuzzy for everyone involved. It doesn't exactly look like the "happily ever after" of every Disney movie about princes and princesses:

For behold, the day is coming, burning like an oven, when all the arrogant and all evildoers will be stubble. The day that is coming shall set them ablaze, says the LORD of hosts, so that it will leave them neither root nor branch. But for you who fear my name, the sun of righteousness shall rise with healing in its wings. You shall go out leaping like calves from the stall. And you shall tread down the wicked, for they will be ashes under the soles of your feet, on the day when I act, says the LORD of hosts. (Mal. 4:1–3)

So "evildoers will be stubble." *Ouch.* "Set ablaze." *Ouch.* This passage says that for those who fear God's name, there will be healing and leaping for joy, but for those who have hated rather than loved God's law, the coming of the King will bring ruin. It seems rather black and white, doesn't it?

In the final verses of the Old Testament in Malachi 4:5–6, we read: "Behold, I will send you Elijah the prophet before the great and awesome day of the LORD comes. And he will turn the hearts of fathers to their children and the hearts of children to their fathers, lest I come and strike the land with a decree of utter destruction."

Consider how the Old Testament began in Genesis 1 with the words over and over again, that God blessed . . . God blessed . . . God blessed. What a contrast from these final verses of the Old Testament. The Old Testament ends not with a blessing, but with a curse, the threat of utter destruction. But there was also hope. God was going to send someone before that "great and awesome day of the LORD." That someone would do a work of turning that would change the way people relate to each other. He would have a message that would confront the status quo, a message that would truly change the world.

But after God spoke through his prophet, Malachi, there was silence for four hundred years. People listened for the voice Isaiah wrote about, and they watched for this messenger Malachi wrote about. Then, finally, an angel appeared to an elderly priest as he carried out his duties in the Holy Place of the temple.

But the angel said to him, "Do not be afraid, Zechariah, for your prayer has been heard, and your wife Elizabeth will bear you a son, and you shall call his name John. And you will have joy and gladness, and many will rejoice at his birth, for he will be great before the Lord. And he must not drink wine or strong drink, and he will be filled with the Holy Spirit, even from his mother's womb. And he will turn many of the children of Israel to the Lord their God, and he will go before him in the spirit and power of Elijah, to turn the hearts of the fathers to the children, and the disobedient to the wisdom of the just, to make ready for the Lord a people prepared." (Luke 1:13–17)

Zechariah knew his Bible. The connection between the angel's words on that day and Malachi's four-hundred-years-ago words must have been obvious to him. The silence was going to be broken. The King was going to come. This son of Zechariah's was going to have a divine mission. He was going to be the voice crying into the wilderness of the world, calling people to get their hearts ready to receive their King!

John's Method

The story of the voice takes a leap forward in Matthew 3.

In those days John the Baptist came preaching in the wilderness of Judea, "Repent, for the kingdom of heaven is at hand." For this is he who was spoken of by the prophet Isaiah when he said,

"The voice of one crying in the wilderness:
'Prepare the way of the Lord;
    make his paths straight.'" (Matt. 3:1–3)

Matthew, the writer of this Gospel, was helping his Jewish readers make the connection between John the Baptist and the person Isaiah and Malachi had promised would come. He wrote:

Now John wore a garment of camel's hair and a leather belt around his waist, and his food was locusts and wild honey. (Matt. 3:4)

What's this about? Why did Matthew include this detail about John's location, wardrobe, and diet? "We're meant to see that John is cut from the same cloth (literally) as the Old Testament prophet, most notably Elijah."[2] John dressed in a way that was similar to Elijah. We're told in 2 Kings 1:8 that Elijah the Tishbite, "wore a garment of hair, with a belt of leather about his waist." John the Baptist wore a coat of camel's hair and a leather belt. During the drought, Elijah lived on stale bread dropped by ravens; John the Baptist spent most of his time in the desert eating locusts and wild honey.

Elijah was a prophet in the days when the king of Israel was actually seeking favor from Beelzebub, the false god of Ekron, instead of the one true God of Israel. His message to the king in his day was, "Now therefore thus says the LORD, you shall not come down from the bed to which you have gone up, but you shall surely die" (2 Kings 1:4). Not exactly a prophetic ray of sunshine!

Like Elijah, John the Baptist also had a challenging message for the people of his day, yet crowds headed out into the wilderness to hear him.

> Then Jerusalem and all Judea and all the region about the Jordan were going out to him, and they were baptized by him in the river Jordan, confessing their sins. (Matt. 3:5–6)

Try to picture this scene. This wasn't everybody heading downtown to hear his or her favorite band. This was everybody leaving the comforts of towns and cities to go out into the wilderness where there were no fast-food offerings, very little water, no bathrooms, and no conveniences. The cities were emptying out, and people were heading into the dry desert. And why were they going? After four hundred years, God had broken his silence and was speaking through the final Old Testament prophet, John. He was out there saying that the day they had been waiting for, the salvation they had been waiting for, the restoration of Israel they had been waiting for, was finally coming!

But John's message also had a bite to it. To be ready for this salvation would require a deep shift in their lives, a costly shift away from the status quo.

John was out there boldly calling God's people to get honest about their sin and confess it. He was calling them to turn away from the sin they had grown comfortable with and set the course of their lives in a radically new direction. He was calling out their hard-heartedness toward God and each other—their presumptions of God's favor based on their bloodline and their prejudice against those who weren't from the "right" bloodline. He was calling them away from empty religiosity to a fuller devotion, away from legalism to love for God's law. He was calling them to turn away from their lack of care and compassion for their aging parents and growing children and instead to turn toward a tenderhearted, big-hearted way of relating to them.

Repentance is never a general thing. Real repentance always requires getting painfully specific regarding sins that we mourn over and turn away from. Someone who occasionally or weekly says, "Forgive us our sins," but never gets specific with God about the jealousy, the greed, the pride that has had a grip on his or her heart that week is not genuinely repentant. But as specific as repentance must be, there is something broader to it. Michael Horton writes,

> Repentance is not modifying a few convictions here and there, but realizing that your whole interpretation of reality—God, yourself, your relation to God and the world—is misguided. It is not finding your way back to the "straight-and-narrow," after wandering off the beaten path a bit, but acknowledging before God that you are not—and never have been—even in the vicinity. You saw yourself at the center of the universe, but now you realize that you exist for God's pleasure and glory, and that changes how you look at everything. The right to determine for yourself what you believe and how you will live is surrendered.[3]

Imagine the men and women wading into the water and listing out loud their sins—their adultery, their hatred, their cruelty, their apathy toward God, their rebellion against God. As they confessed their sins, wanting to come clean and remain clean, they followed John into the waters of baptism, which symbolized the washing away of sins. Baptism wasn't new to these people. Baptism was one of the rituals that Gentiles who wanted to embrace Judaism went through. But these weren't Gentiles that John was baptizing. They were Jews. In calling them into the Jordan to be baptized, John was suggesting to these Jews that they were lost sinners, in need of salvation. Imagine the humility that John's baptism required of a Jew. By this act, she was confessing the inadequacy of her religious heritage to save her from her sins. She was placing herself on the same (lower) level, the same kingdom-outsider status, as a Gentile.

The Jordan was the river her forefathers crossed to enter into the promised land. She and her neighbors were going back into it because they found themselves on the brink of a new era for the people of God, and they wanted to be all in. They didn't want to miss it. They wanted to be washed and waiting for their King's arrival.

But it was not just those who were willing to repent who were going out to hear what John had to say.

> But when he saw many of the Pharisees and Sadducees coming to his baptism, he said to them, "You brood of vipers! Who warned you to flee from the wrath to come? Bear fruit in keeping with repentance. And do not presume to say to yourselves, 'We have Abraham as our father,' for I tell you, God is able from these stones to raise up children for Abraham. Even now the axe is laid to the root of the trees. Every tree therefore that does not bear good fruit is cut down and thrown into the fire." (Matt. 3:7–10)

These Pharisees and Sadducees, the religious elite of their day, weren't coming to be baptized; they came to observe and condemn the baptism John was performing there. They had worked hard to convince their Jewish followers that simply being Jewish and keeping the law (as they interpreted it) was sufficient to make them acceptable to God. John's ministry and message—and now, this baptism of his—suggested otherwise.

Real repentance doesn't come naturally, even to—and perhaps especially to—religious people. It takes a great deal of humility to say, "I've been wrong. I've been going in the wrong direction, and now, with all the strength God gives me, I intend to go in the opposite direction—toward dependence instead of independence, toward living to please God instead of just using God, toward humble obedience instead of prideful resistance." Repentance is not just a tweak. It's not a slight adjustment on the compass. It is a full turn that proves itself to be genuine by the fruit that is borne in a person's life.

There was no repentance and, therefore, no fruit of genuine repentance in the lives of the presumptuous, hypocritical religious elite who came out to the wilderness to condemn John. So John asked them, "Who warned you to flee from the wrath to come?" (v. 7). He was prompting them to remember the verses they had learned in Sabbath school. Their answer should have been: "The prophet Isaiah." It was Isaiah who had used the imagery of axes being laid at the root of trees to warn God's people of his coming wrath:

> Behold, the Lord GOD of hosts
>   will lop the boughs with terrifying power;
> the great in height will be hewn down,
>   and the lofty will be brought low.
> He will cut down the thickets of the forest with an axe,
>   and Lebanon will fall by the Majestic One. (Isa. 10:33–34)

It was Isaiah who wrote about being thrown into the fire:

> And they shall go out and look on the dead bodies of the men
> who have rebelled against me. For their worm shall not die,

their fire shall not be quenched, and they shall be an abhor-
rence to all flesh. (Isa. 66:24)

It was rigid and prideful resistance to repentance that made these
religious leaders vulnerable to God's wrath. But they didn't see
themselves as vulnerable to this judgment; they saw themselves
as protected from this judgment. They were like many people
today who are so busy with church activities, or people who went
through a religious ritual in their childhood who are confident
that they're "in," even though there is no fruit of genuine repentance and faith in their lives.

And I just have to stop to ask: Are you vulnerable? Is there fruit
of genuine repentance in your life? The fruit of repentance from
bitterness in the form of forgiveness? The fruit of repentance from
greed in the form of increasing generosity? The fruit of repentance from self-centeredness in the form of being more concerned
about the needs and hurts of others than about your own needs
and hurts? Has there been a radical reorientation in your life that
has put Christ at the center and not just at the fringes?

While John's baptism was meaningful, he knew that it was
not everything God's people needed. It was merely preparatory
for something that only the King he came to herald could provide. "I baptize you with water for repentance, but he who is
coming after me is mightier than I, whose sandals I am not worthy to carry. He will baptize you with the Holy Spirit and fire"
(Matt. 3:11).

John knew that his outward baptism was merely symbolic of
an inner cleansing. There was one coming who could accomplish
that inner cleansing with a purifying fire, one coming who could
make spiritually dead people alive. His water baptism was simply
a symbol; the Spirit's baptism would be the reality that the symbol
pointed toward.

But then, someone came to be baptized by John who needed no
cleansing, no repentance:

Then Jesus came from Galilee to the Jordan to John, to be baptized by him. John would have prevented him, saying, "I need to be baptized by you, and do you come to me?" But Jesus answered him, "Let it be so now, for thus it is fitting for us to fulfill all righteousness." Then he consented. And when Jesus was baptized, immediately he went up from the water, and behold, the heavens were opened to him, and he saw the Spirit of God descending like a dove and coming to rest on him; and behold, a voice from heaven said, "This is my beloved Son, with whom I am well pleased." (Matt. 3:13–17)

Why would Jesus come to John to be baptized? And what did he mean that this act was "fitting . . . to fulfill all righteousness"? Evidently, there was something Jesus and John had to do in order to fulfill the plan of God, and part of that plan was brought about by Jesus receiving John's baptism.

In the Old Testament, baptism was a form of consecration. When a priest reached the age of entry to public ministry at age thirty, he was baptized, set apart. So in his baptism, Jesus was being consecrated for service. Of course, at the heart of Jesus's service to God was his identification with God's people. He had taken on flesh and entered into the world, and now he was wading into the waters of baptism to step even further into identifying with us and our need—our need for cleansing from sin, and ultimately, our need for someone to bear the punishment for our sin. It was as he approached John for baptism that John recognized that was exactly who Jesus was. We read in John 1,

He saw Jesus coming toward him, and said, "Behold, the Lamb of God, who takes away the sin of the world! This is he of whom I said, 'After me comes a man who ranks before me, because he was before me.' I myself did not know him, but for this purpose I came baptizing with water, that he might be revealed to Israel." (John 1:29–31)

There at the Jordan, John recognized Jesus as the sin-bearer, the Lamb who would be slain. There in the Jordan, as Jesus emerged from the waters of baptism, Jesus was revealed, not only to John, but to all who heard the voice of God himself from heaven identifying Jesus as his Son, as the King who came to usher in God's kingdom, as the servant God spoke about through the prophet Isaiah when he wrote:

> Behold my servant, whom I uphold,
>> my chosen, in whom my soul delights [*in whom I am well pleased*];
> I have put my Spirit upon him [*visibly*];
>> he will bring forth justice to the nations. (Isa. 42:1)

Surely John made the connection between God's words spoken from heaven at Jesus's baptism and this passage in Isaiah 42. Jesus would be the one who would "bring forth justice." That's what John and so many others were counting on. Finally, the King had come who would put an end to the tyranny and oppression brought upon Israel by so many foreign powers.

But then, as Jesus began his ministry in Galilee preaching on a hillside, multiplying fish and bread, and healing people with diseases, John didn't see Jesus bringing forth justice. In fact, a short time later, John found himself languishing in prison under a ruler who was thoroughly corrupt and cruel. Jesus didn't seem to be living up to what John understood from the Scriptures that the Christ would be and do. Jesus wasn't living up to John's expectations. Some of us know just what that's like. But unlike some of us, who perhaps become angry or alienated from Jesus when he doesn't do what we expect him to do, John went straight to Jesus with his questions.

John's Misunderstanding

> Now when John heard in prison about the deeds of the Christ, he sent word by his disciples and said to him, "Are you the one who is to come, or shall we look for another?" (Matt. 11:2–3)

John's problem with Jesus was not one rooted in unbelief or emotional frailty under pressure. John's concern was based on the fact that from his vantage point, Jesus did not seem to be fulfilling the Scriptures. From his many years spent out in the wilderness, living and breathing the Old Testament scriptures, John had seen clearly that when the Christ came, he would set things right in the world. He would punish wrong and reward right. John's message to the people of his day—based on the Scriptures—had been that the "axe is laid to the root of the trees," but he was hearing reports of Jesus cleansing a leper, healing a centurion's servant, and casting demons out of man. Imagine the evil things this man with a demon must have done in his community that deserved judgment, not mercy. John began to wonder: *Where is the axe, and when is Jesus going to start swinging it?*

There was something in the Old Testament scriptures that was not clear to John, something that created a misunderstanding as he waited in prison for the winnowing fork to begin gathering the chaff to set it on fire. John the Baptist, like most of the prophets and like so many people of his day, did not understand that the Christ would come twice: the first time to proclaim his kingdom and die as a once-for-all sacrifice for sinners, and the second time to establish his kingdom and destroy his enemies. John was expecting everything promised by the prophets of the Old Testament to take place in one monumental day of the Lord in his first coming.

> And Jesus answered them, "Go and tell John what you hear and see: the blind receive their sight and the lame walk, lepers are cleansed and the deaf hear, and the dead are raised up, and the poor have good news preached to them. And blessed is the one who is not offended by me." (Matt. 11:4–6)

Jesus knew that John's doubts were based on his understanding of the Scripture, so he used that very Scripture to address John's misunderstanding. He knew John was familiar with Isaiah 35, which says:

Behold, your God
    will come with vengeance,
with the recompense of God.
    He will come and save you. (v. 4)

These words had shaped John's expectations. But the passage continued:

Then the eyes of the blind shall be opened,
    and the ears of the deaf unstopped;
then shall the lame man leap like a deer,
    and the tongue of the mute sing for joy. (vv. 5–6)

John needed to be reminded of the promised healing ministry of the Messiah, not just his promised vengeance. Jesus knew John was familiar with Isaiah 61's proclamation of "the day of vengeance of our God," but before that day, according to Isaiah 61, was to be a day of bringing good news to the poor, a day of binding up the brokenhearted, a day of proclaiming the Lord's favor. Jesus took John right to passages where the judgment of the Messiah is stressed and pointed him to the parts of those passages that speak of the Messiah's ministry of healing and blessing and proclaiming good news. It wasn't yet time for an axe. It wasn't yet time for fire. John needed to wait for the entire drama of redemptive history to unfold.

But of course, John would not be around to witness the event that is at the center of redemptive history. John would not be around to see with his eyes the suffering servant of Isaiah 53 pierced for our transgressions, crushed for our iniquities. Though John had recognized Jesus to be the Lamb of God who takes away the sin of the world, he would not live to see Isaiah 53's Lamb led to slaughter, cut off from the land of the living, and stricken for the transgression of his people. John didn't fully understand that in his first coming, Jesus came, not to judge sinners but to bear sin. Jesus came not to punish transgressors but to be numbered among them. John was like all the other Old Testament prophets who, according to 1 Peter 1, "searched and inquired carefully, inquiring what person or time the Spirit of Christ in them was indicating when he predicted the sufferings of Christ and the subsequent glories" (1 Pet. 1:10–11).

John the Baptist couldn't see the suffering and glory of Jesus as clearly as you and I can today on this side of the cross, resurrection, and ascension. In fact, this is what Jesus was getting at when he said in Matthew 11:11: "Among those born of women there has arisen no one greater than John the Baptist. Yet the one who is least in the kingdom of heaven is greater than he." John the Baptist was the greatest of the prophets because he didn't merely search and inquire about the Christ; he saw and experienced the Christ in his lifetime, which no other Old Testament prophet had ever done. But you and I and every believer who lives on this side of Pentecost are greater than John the Baptist because we haven't just read about and anticipated being given the new heart of flesh that the prophet Ezekiel wrote about—we've experienced it.

Herod's Missed Opportunity

John had his heart set on the kingdom of God and the coming King. He longed for him to set things right in this world. John had his mind filled with God's word, even if he didn't understand it perfectly or completely. But if we are tempted to think that the saintliness of John meant he would be immune from the cruelty of scoundrels, we are sorely mistaken.

> For it was Herod who had sent and seized John and bound him in prison for the sake of Herodias, his brother Philip's wife, because he had married her. For John had been saying to Herod, "It is not lawful for you to have your brother's wife." And Herodias had a grudge against him and wanted to put him to death. But she could not, for Herod feared John, knowing that he was a righteous and holy man, and he kept him safe. When he heard him, he was greatly perplexed, and yet he heard him gladly. (Mark 6:17–20)

The name "Herod" is mentioned nearly fifty times in the New Testament, but the name refers to a number of different men. Understanding this mixed-up family takes a little effort. The Herods mentioned in the New Testament were all part of a dynasty of rulers who were set over Judea by the Roman Empire in 40 BC. They were descendants of Esau, not Jacob, but their ancestors had converted to Judaism. When the New Testament opens, we meet Herod the Great, and he was out to kill Jesus. You can imagine that a man who was willing to kill every male child under the age of two, just to make sure he got the one who posed a threat to him, was not the nicest of guys or the most nurturing of dads. Toward the end of his reign, thinking his own family was out to overthrow him, Herod the Great murdered one of his wives, her mother, his brother-in-law, and three of his sons. After Herod the Great's death, his living sons (Herod Archelaus, Herod Antipas, and Herod Philip) split control of the region of Palestine. Herod Archelaus was placed over Judea, Samaria, and Idumea but was removed two years later. Herod Philip ruled over the Gaulanitis (the Golan Heights, east of the Jordan River). Herod Antipas ruled over Galilee. Herod Antipas is the Herod here in our passage.

Early in his reign, Herod Antipas married an Arabian princess. But on a visit to Rome, where he stayed with his half-brother, Herod Philip, he fell in love (or at least lust) with his brother's wife, Herodias. They each divorced their spouses so they could marry each other. Now if all the brothers have names that start with Herod and one of them marries someone named Herodias, what does that suggest to you? Yes, this was an incestuous marriage, as Herodias was not only this Herod's brother's wife, she was also this Herod's niece.

And then along came John, a man whose whole life was oriented around calling people to repentance and faith. His message was that the kingdom of God was at hand, and even Herod would have to bow to the divine King and should prepare for his coming through repentance. John took God's word and obedience to it quite seriously. And here was Herod, the appointed leader over God's people, flagrantly disobeying Leviticus 18:16, which says, "You shall not uncover the nakedness of your brother's wife," as well as disobeying the seventh commandment: "You shall not commit adultery" (Ex. 20:14).

Why couldn't John just look the other way? Why couldn't he just preach a nice sermon about the power of love and how it can change the world? Didn't he understand these two people were soul mates and that their love could not be denied? Apparently not. John was, according to Mark 6:20, "a righteous and holy man." He loved what was right and hated what was evil. Notice the text says in verse 18, "John *had been saying* to Herod, it is not lawful for you to have your brother's wife." It seems as though this was more than a one-time confrontation. But Herod and Herodias had no interest in obeying God; no interest in a repentance that would require that they say no to their romantic, relational, and sexual desires. They just wanted to follow their hearts and not God's law. They had the opportunity to repent and be reconciled to God through the ministry of John the Baptist. They could have had their sins forgiven and made a fresh start. But instead, they dug in. And evidently John refused to let it go. His repeated calls to repentance made Herodias so mad, she wanted to kill John and began looking for an opportunity to do it.

> But an opportunity came when Herod on his birthday gave a banquet for his nobles and military commanders and the lead-ing men of Galilee. For when Herodias's daughter came in and danced, she pleased Herod and his guests. And the king said to the girl, "Ask me for whatever you wish, and I will give it to you." And he vowed to her, "Whatever you ask me, I will give you, up to half of my kingdom." And she went out and said to her mother, "For what should I ask?" And she said, "The head of John the Baptist." And she came in immediately with haste to the king and asked, saying, "I want you to give me at once the head of John the Baptist on a platter." And the king was exceedingly sorry, but because of his oaths and his guests he

did not want to break his word to her. And immediately the king sent an executioner with orders to bring John's head. He went and beheaded him in the prison and brought his head on a platter and gave it to the girl, and the girl gave it to her mother. (Mark 6:21–28)

Herod had invited all the big shots from around Galilee to his birthday party. But this banquet was more like a bachelor party. When Herodias's daughter came in and danced, and we read that she "pleased" Herod and his guests, I think we're meant to imagine this scene in all its sickening sensuality. Herod was aroused by his young stepdaughter—so aroused he was not thinking clearly and made a crazy promise. This promise presented Herodias with the opportunity she had been looking for to silence the voice—the voice of one crying in the wilderness, the voice that had been preaching in the palace: "Prepare the way of the Lord; make his paths straight." An opportunity presented itself, and she was ready to take it. However, what she saw as her opportunity to silence John the Baptist's voice was really her final opportunity to repent. Sadly, it was a missed opportunity.

The voice calling for preparation for judgment through confession of sin and repentance was silenced by a pair of scoundrels bent on having their own way.

On the night that Jesus was arrested, the religious leaders took him to Pilate, the Roman governor over Judea. Pilate didn't know what to do with this Jesus, in whom he found no guilt. But then he heard that Jesus had been teaching in Galilee and decided he would rid himself of this problem prisoner by sending him to the Roman ruler over Galilee, Herod Antipas, who happened to be in Jerusalem that night.

When Herod saw Jesus, he was very glad, for he had long desired to see him, because he had heard about him, and he was hoping to see some sign done by him. So he questioned him at some length, but he made no answer. (Luke 23:8–9)

Herod had loved keeping John around to hear him preach, even though Herod had no intention of responding in repentance to John's preaching. A short time later, this same fascination with spiritual things had Herod wanting to see Jesus. He wanted to see Jesus do one of those miracles he'd heard about, even though Herod again had no intention of opening up his life to a miracle accomplished in his own heart through repentance and faith.

The voice had confronted Herod again and again, beckoning him toward repentance, but Herod had resisted and refused again and again. He repeatedly silenced the voice of conviction when John was alive and then silenced the voice of conviction for good by ending John's life. And now, here was Jesus standing before him, and Jesus was unwilling to speak at all. Jesus knew Herod had no interest in humbling himself and was merely seeking to amuse himself. Sadly, as Jesus refused to speak, it became clear that Herod had missed his opportunity to repent.

> The chief priests and the scribes stood by, vehemently accusing [Jesus]. And Herod with his soldiers treated him with contempt and mocked him. Then, arraying him in splendid clothing, he sent him back to Pilate. (Luke 23:10–11)

+ John had used his voice to proclaim the coming of the Christ, while Herod used his voice to mock Christ.
+ John's heart was filled with joy in Jesus's presence, while Herod's heart was filled with contempt in Jesus's presence.
+ John invested his life in preparing people to come under the rule of King Jesus, while Herod wasted his life mocking the rule of King Jesus.

John the Baptist and Herod present us with a stark contrast that should prompt us to turn our gaze inward, into the condition of our own hearts and lives. It should bring us to ask ourselves:

+ Is my heart set on the kingdom of God, or am I too busy building my own kingdom?
+ Am I putting myself under the authority of God's word, or am I merely entertained by God's word?
+ Is my life bearing fruit in keeping with repentance, or is it bearing fruit in keeping with rebellion?
+ Is my life marked by the fruit of the Spirit, or is it driven by the lust of the flesh?
+ Am I pursuing holiness in light of the coming judgment, or am I presuming upon protection in the coming judgment?
+ Am I confessing my guilt so that my conscience is cleansed, or have I simmered in guilt so that my conscience has become seared?

Herod's missed opportunity stands as a warning to every person who hears the gospel and toys with it instead of taking hold of it. Herod's missed opportunity stands as a warning to every person who might be interested in hearing Bible teaching but has no intention to let it change her; no intention to allow it to interfere in how she uses her power, her money, her sexuality, and her time; and no intention of allowing it to disrupt the status quo of her life. My friend, resist the conviction of the Holy Spirit at great peril—the peril that your conscience will become seared by your own repeated resistance so that you can no longer feel it being pricked anymore. What a tragedy to resist the call of Christ for so long that the day comes when his voice is silenced in your life.

When John the Baptist came to Herod as a voice speaking into the wilderness that was Herod's life, Herod's home, and Herod's heart, Herod could have humbled himself and separated himself from his incestuous relationship with Herodias. Herod could have bowed to the true King, Jesus Christ, and been transformed. He could have experienced the baptism by fire, a baptism that changes a spiritually dead person into a spiritually alive person. But he loved his sin way too much. He loved his autonomy way too much. He had no interest in the humbling required to say,

"I've been wrong about pretty much everything, and everything in my life is going to have to be reordered around Jesus beginning today." The day came for Herod when, after having said "no" to the word of God that he had heard again and again, after having again and again doused the glimmer of hope that he could actually live a new life of holiness rather than one filled with shame, Jesus no longer spoke to him.

John's call is really the Spirit of God's call to respond to the reality of the coming of Jesus by clearing the way for him in your own heart and life through repentance. Next time, Jesus will come in judgment. Next time, the axe will fall; the fire will burn.

Don't say you'll do something about this later. Later, the opportunity might be gone.

Don't hold on so tight to whatever sin you think you can't live without that you do not take hold of Jesus.

Come to the waters that cleanse. Confess and be forgiven.

You don't have to live in fear of the axe at the root of the tree of your life or the fire that would burn away the chaff of your life. Instead, you can live in glad expectation of the coming of the King, knowing that you are prepared for his coming through repentance and faith.

> Rock of Ages, cleft for me,
> Let me hide myself in thee;
> Let the water and the blood,
> From thy wounded side which flowed,
> Be of sin the double cure;
> Save from wrath and make me pure.
>
> Not the labors of my hands
> Can fulfill thy law's demands;
> Could my zeal no respite know,
> Could my tears forever flow,
> All for sin could not atone;
> Thou must save, and thou alone.

Nothing in my hand I bring,
Simply to the cross I cling;
Naked, come to thee for dress;
Helpless, look to thee for grace;
Foul, I to the fountain fly;
Wash me, Savior, or I die.[4]

2

THE FAMILY

When we moved to Nashville in 1993, people started asking us if we were related to the Guthries who lived in the area. We always said "no" because David's family was all from the Pacific Northwest, not Tennessee. Or . . . so we thought. Last year, David decided to sign up for a two-week free trial on Ancestry.com, and he traced his line back to Henry Guthrie. This Henry Guthrie fought in the Revolutionary War in North Carolina and then was one of the first settlers of Fort Nashborough, which eventually became Nashville. He was one of 256 signers of the Cumberland Compact, the precursor to Tennessee's state constitution. He was buried just a few miles from where we live today. If we want to pay $25, we could have our names added to the list of "First Families of Tennessee" and receive a "handsomely designed certificate" to display.

I hope you're impressed. We are very impressed with ourselves.

Honestly, while I've never been that interested in trying to trace my own ancestry, I do enjoy watching the television shows like *Who Do You Think You Are?* on TLC or *Finding Your Roots* on PBS where various celebrities trace their ancestry. With the aid of census data, birth/marriage/death records, old newspaper stories, museum archives, and sometimes DNA testing, featured celebrities often discover that they have descended from noteworthy, admirable, even royal ancestors. But they also often discover ancestors who did cruel, contemptible, even criminal, things. Some find abolitionists in their history, while others find slaves or slaveholders (or even former slaves who became slaveholders themselves!). Some find ancestors who fought for noble causes, while others discover ancestors who fought for what our modern sensibilities suggest was the wrong side.

What I find fascinating is the way the celebrities want to be able to connect certain aspects of their own lives to something in their ancestors. Musical artists are thrilled to find musicianship in their ancestral history. Those who have persevered through difficulty want to find perseverance in their ancestors. Oftentimes they take great pride in the accomplishments and character of their ancestors. Other times they experience great sorrow and even shame over who their ancestors were and what they did.

In this chapter, we're going to take a look at Jesus's family—his ancestors, his parents, and his siblings—to see what they reveal to us about who Jesus is and what it means to be in his family. In reality, we all want and need to be adopted into his family so that we can call God our Father and call Jesus our brother. If there are particular traits of those who are part of Jesus's family, we want to be able to see those traits in our own lives.

Jesus's Ancestors

Jesus did not need the producers of one of these television shows, a DNA test, or a computer program to trace his ancestry. The Gospel writers Matthew and Luke did it for him. In fact, Matthew begins his Gospel this way: "The book of the genealogy of Jesus Christ, the son of David, the son of Abraham" (Matt. 1:1). From there, Matthew traces the legal descent of Jesus in three groupings of fourteen generations, allowing himself to make omissions.

Why did Matthew begin his Gospel this way? Matthew was writing to the Jews whose lives revolved around promises God made to their ancestors. God had promised Abraham that he would be the father of many nations, and that through him and his family, all the nations of the earth would be blessed (Gen. 12:3). Hundreds of years later, one of Abraham's descendants, David, became the king over Israel, and God made incredible promises to him as well. God promised David that his descendants would be a great dynasty of kings and that one particular son of his would rule on his throne—not just for a few years, and not even for a lifetime, but forever. That son, he was promised, would not merely rule over the twelve tribes of Israel but would also rule the nations (2 Sam. 7:12–16; Ps. 2:8). These promises to Abraham and David were incredible promises, and they were connected promises. Evidently, the way that all the families of the earth would be blessed would be through a kingdom ruled forever by a son of David.

These promises seemed to be becoming a reality when David's son Solomon came to the throne. But, as wise as Solomon was, he did some very foolish things. Then when Solomon's son Rehoboam took the throne, the kingdom split, and it was never again as glorious as it had been. The day even came when no descendant of David was seated on the throne over Israel. In fact, eventually, there was no throne in Israel. In the days when Matthew wrote his Gospel, the people of Israel were living under a puppet ruler put in place by Rome. It did not look like the promises God made to Abraham and David were ever going to become a reality.

By beginning his Gospel with this genealogy, Matthew declared that the Jesus who was born in Bethlehem, raised by Joseph, and who worked as a craftsman in Nazareth was the descendant of Abraham through whom all the nations of the earth would be blessed. Matthew sought to convince his readers that Jesus, who had no home, no fortune, and only an unimpressive group of followers, was the royal King in the line of David whose kingdom would never end.

But honestly, if that was all that Matthew was trying to accomplish, he could have gone about recording Jesus's family history in a very different way. If that's all Matthew was trying to communicate, there would be no reason for him to include some of the names he chose to include in the genealogy, specifically the names of five women.

Jewish genealogies (and most genealogies in the Bible) don't include women. But more interesting than the fact that Matthew included women is the particular women he chose to include and to leave out. We might expect Matthew, writing for a Jewish audience, to include Jewish matriarchs such as Sarah, Rebekah, or Leah. But of the five women Matthew included in Jesus's genealogy, four aren't even Jewish. Only Mary, who likely descended from the kingly line of David like her husband, Joseph, was Jewish. The other four women Matthew took care to include in Jesus's genealogy were Gentiles! Tamar and Rahab were Canaanites, the race of people living in Canaan when the Israelites took possession of the land. Ruth was a Moabite. Then there was Bathsheba, who, though she may have been an Israelite by birth, was married to Uriah the Hittite, which legally made her a Hittite.

Matthew seems to be going out of his way to make clear to his Jewish readers that God had always intended for his blessings, his promises, his rule to be for people from every tribe, tongue, and nation—not exclusively for those who had pure Jewish blood in their veins. It seems as if Matthew wanted to make clear that being a part of the people of God, the family of God, has never been about blood but has always been about belief. It is about taking hold of the promises God made to Abraham, Isaac, and Jacob, which is exactly what Tamar, Rahab, and Ruth did.

That Matthew included women who were foreigners in his genealogy is not the only thing that stands out when we read it. We can't escape the reality that the lives of each of the women he chose to include were touched by sexual scandal.

Tamar's first husband was so evil that God put him death. Imagine being married to a man that evil! Left a childless widow, Tamar, following the cultural practices of her time, married her husband's brother, but this brother didn't want to share his inheritance with children born to her, so he simply used Tamar for his sexual pleasure while avoiding impregnating her. God put him to death for his evil ways too. Left widowed again and desperate for security and posterity, Tamar dressed as a temple prostitute and put herself in the path of her father-in-law, Judah. Evidently, she knew Judah was such a lowlife, he would easily be seduced. She also knew she would need evidence of their liaison to keep from being killed once her pregnancy was discovered, so she kept his seal and staff. And her plan worked. She gave birth to twins fathered by her father-in-law. And one of her twins, Perez, became part of Jesus's family tree. (For Tamar's story, see Genesis 38.)

Then there was Rahab (see Joshua 2 and 6). She was running a brothel in Jericho when the advance party of two million invading Israelites came to her town and to her inn. She had heard about how their God gave them victory over their enemies, and she knew that the city of Jericho was the next enemy to be defeated. She wanted into the Israelite family and was not only saved by Israelites, she became one of them through marriage. The former madam became a mother and a grandmother, also finding a place in the lineage of Jesus (Matt. 1:3).

Ruth was a Moabite. That meant she traced her ancestry, not to Abraham but to his nephew Lot. Do you remember Lot? He was the guy who impregnated his daughters while drunk. This was the incestuous family and culture Ruth came from. A Jewish family escaping famine in their hometown of Bethlehem moved to Moab, and she married one of their sons. But then he died, leaving her a childless widow. Eventually, she traveled to Bethlehem with her mother-in-law, Naomi, where she was resented as "the Moabitess" by most of the Bethlehem folks. But a godly man named Boaz called her "my daughter," and eventually, "my wife." Thus, Ruth, a foreigner brought into the family, became a great-grandmother to David, whose greater son would be Jesus (see Ruth 1–4).

Matthew calls Bathsheba "the wife of Uriah" to remind readers of two things: (1) she was a Hittite by marriage, and (2) she was married to Uriah when David summoned her to his bedroom. Hers is a story of being used sexually, which led to an unexpected pregnancy (see 2 Samuel 11–12). But she too, through her son Solomon, found her way into the family of Jesus (Matt. 1:6).

All the sexual scandal in the lives of these women prepares us for the great scandal to come: the pregnancy of unwed Mary, the mother of Jesus. Though Mary had not committed any sexual sin herself, she was likely shunned by her pious neighbors as she carried the unborn Christ in her womb.

If the producers of *Who Do You Think You Are?* were looking for ancestors to include in Jesus's story, the lives of these five women would make great television. But why would Matthew include them in his Gospel? It would seem that Matthew used the genealogy of Jesus to make it abundantly clear:

The family of Jesus is made up of people who come from less-than-respectable backgrounds and have less-than-perfect records.

Jesus came from a long line of outsiders, outlaws, scoundrels, and sinners. When he entered into the world, he entered into the messiness of the human family, even in his own family. In fact, he was the only member of this family who never brought shame upon the family. Instead, he took upon himself the shame of every person in the family tree. Think of Abraham's shame for allowing his fears to put his wife in a compromising situation. Jesus bore that shame as he hung on the cross even though Jesus always protects his bride. Think of Jacob's shame for a lifetime of deception. Jesus bore that shame, though he always told the truth and, in fact, is the Truth. Think of Judah's shame over selling his brother (Joseph) to slave traders, lying to his grieving father (Jacob) for years, and his incestuous liaison with his son's wife (Tamar). Jesus, the Lion of the tribe of Judah, took upon himself the sin and shame of Judah. Think of King David's shame over taking another man's wife into his own bed and then organizing her husband's murder. Jesus bore that shame as he hung on the cross under a hastily made, mocking sign that read, "King of the Jews." Jesus came to save both victim and perpetrator, sinner and sinned against.

As we consider the kind of people who are part of the family of Jesus, I can't help but ask, Is there something in your own story that makes you think you could never belong in God's family? Has a sense of shame shaped your sense of self so that you think your name will not be found on that list of names of those whom Jesus calls beloved brothers and sisters? My friend, if the story and secrets of your life were recorded for all to read, as the stories of Abraham and Sarah, Judah and Tamar, Rahab, Ruth, or David and Bathsheba were recorded for us to read—if your story includes sexual scandal such as adultery, incest, or becoming pregnant by someone you're not married to—you're going to fit right in to this family. If you've been deceitful or hateful . . . if you've used or destroyed other people to get what you wanted . . . if you've touted your religious credentials to impress other people when in reality you wanted nothing to do with God himself, welcome to the family! If you've taken God's generous provision to you for granted . . . if you've doubted God's promises . . . if you've presumed upon God's protection while also ignoring him—we can see the family resemblance. If you have no hope to be accepted into God's family other than the perfect record of your righteous brother, Jesus, then you can be sure you've found your forever-family. No one gets into God's family by being born into it. You must be reborn into it. And no one gets into God's family through good behavior. The only way any of us become a part of this family is by grace through faith.

> Grace, grace, God's grace,
> Grace that will pardon and cleanse within;
> Grace, grace, God's grace,
> Grace that is greater than all our sin.[5]

"The saying is trustworthy and deserving of full acceptance, that Christ Jesus came into the world to save sinners" (1 Tim. 1:15). Matthew wanted us to see that the family of Jesus was made up of people who had less-than-perfect records. This means that there is hope, there is a home, there is a future in this family for people like me and people like you—no matter what we've done or failed to do, or who we've been or failed to be.

Jesus's Parents

When we're introduced to Joseph, who would be Jesus's earthly adopted father, we find him to be the kind of person we all want to have as our father, our brother, or our husband.

> Now the birth of Jesus Christ took place in this way. When his mother Mary had been betrothed to Joseph, before they came together she was found to be with child from the Holy Spirit. And her husband Joseph, being a just man and unwilling to put her to shame, resolved to divorce her quietly. (Matt. 1:18–19)

We learn two things about Joseph here. He was a just man. In other words, he cared about justice. He cared about doing what was right. He loved the law of God and wanted to live by it. The problem was that, from his vantage point, Mary had been party to a great wrong. She was pregnant, and he knew he was not the father. To begin their life together as if she had not slept with another man would be ignoring God's law.

But Joseph was not just concerned with justice and righteousness. He was kind. He didn't want Mary's pregnant picture splashed on the cover of the tabloids in a way that would humiliate her. So he decided to do his best to make it a quiet divorce, and then he went to bed. Then an angel of the Lord appeared to him in a dream, addressing him this way: "Joseph, son of David." It was as if the angel was reminding Joseph that he was in the royal line, the one the forever king was supposed to come from. The angel seemed to want Joseph to think of the news he was about to receive in light of God's promise to David.

The angel said, "Do not fear to take Mary as your wife, for that which is conceived in her is from the Holy Spirit" (Matt. 1:20). There was nothing that made this explanation easier for Joseph to believe than it would be for us to believe today. He knew the birds and the bees. He was asked to believe that Mary was pregnant, not by another man but by the Holy Spirit, and that this child was going to be the Savior that his people had been watching and waiting for ever since those promises were made to Abraham and David—really, ever since the promise was made to the serpent in Eden: that one day a descendant would be born who would crush the serpent's head and put an end to his evil. "She [Mary] will bear a son, and you shall call his name Jesus, for he will save his people from their sins" (Matt. 1:20–21). Joseph was told that this baby would be the savior of his people. He would save them, not from the physical oppression of the Roman occupying forces but from the spiritual enslavement of sin.

Matthew continues, "When Joseph woke from sleep, he did as the angel of the Lord commanded him: he took his wife, but knew her not until she had given birth to a son. And he called his name Jesus" (Matt. 1:24–25).

Joseph demonstrated what Jesus would later say is a family trait of all those who are adopted into his family. Joseph heard the word of God, and he obeyed.

And he was not the only one.

When the angel Gabriel told Mary (who was betrothed to Joseph but had never slept with him or any man) that she was going to conceive and bear a son, she understandably asked how this would happen. The angel answered, "The Holy Spirit will come upon you, and the power of the Most High will overshadow you; therefore the child to be born will be called holy—the Son of God" (Luke 1:35).

Mary's response, similar to Joseph's response, was stunning: "And Mary said, 'Behold, I am the servant of the Lord; let it be to me according to your word'" (Luke 1:38). She had heard God's word, and she intended to submit to it and obey it no matter what it might cost her. And, oh, it would cost her.

But because she really believed that God at work in and through her life was cause for joy, she was full of joy—joy that erupted into song. In her song, Mary quoted or alluded to verses from Genesis, Deuteronomy, 1 and 2 Samuel, Job, Psalms, Isaiah, Ezekiel, Micah, Habakkuk, and Zephaniah. Mary knew God's word. Her life had clearly been saturated in it. In her song, she connected the promises made to Abraham and to David with the baby she was carrying:

> He [the Lord] has helped his servant Israel,
> > in remembrance of his mercy,
> as he spoke to our fathers,
> > to Abraham and to his offspring forever. (Luke 1:54–55)

We read that "Mary treasured up all these things, pondering them in her heart" (Luke 2:19). There were things she understood about her child, Jesus, but there were also things she did not yet understand. She was pondering. She was trying to put two and two together. There was a sense in which she and Joseph understood that Jesus was divine, that he was destined to set things right in the world, that he was the king in the line of David promised by God. But there was also a sense in which they didn't understand. They had a less-than-complete understanding of who Jesus was.

Jesus was a fully human baby. There was no glow around him like we see in classic paintings. While changing his diapers and watching him learn to walk and talk, perhaps it was easy for Mary and Joseph to forget, at times, who Jesus really was. Jesus "increased in wisdom" (Luke 2:52). He didn't come out of the womb knowing everything. They had to teach him. He had to learn.

As Jesus learned to read and began to study the scrolls that contained the writings of Moses and the Prophets, Jesus grew from a lesser to a greater understanding of God's plan to redeem all things through Christ. He grew in his understanding of his own identity as the Christ.

So let me ask you this: If Jesus had to grow in his understanding of his own identity and mission, doesn't it make sense that you and I would have to grow in our understanding of his identity and mission? Every one of us who comes to him and takes hold of him does so without having figured out everything about him. Every one of us who puts our faith in him does so in faith, seeking understanding.

Don't think that you have to have everything about Jesus figured out before you put your trust in him. You don't.

The family of Jesus is made up of people who have a less-than-complete understanding of who he is and what he is doing in the world.

For most of us, the recognition of who Jesus is comes gradually. We have a sense of "I get it, but I don't get it." Personally, I have to say (as someone whose earliest memories include being taught about Jesus and as someone who has spent almost six decades learning about him) that while there is much I understand about Jesus and his purposes in the world, there is still so much I don't understand. I still have so much to learn. I still have so much more clarity to anticipate on that day when faith becomes sight.

Jesus's Siblings

It took Mary a long time to fully grasp the gospel centered in her son. She didn't always understand who he was or what he was doing. Yet we know that Mary came to not only love Jesus as her son, but to worship him as her Savior. We find her gathered with the early believers to worship God and wait for the promised Holy Spirit after Jesus's ascension (Acts 1:14). In fact, it was not just Mary, Jesus's mother, who was there; his brothers were there too. Perhaps it is easy to read quickly over this statement in Acts 1, but if we trace the story of Jesus's family through the Gospels, it's rather surprising.

The Gospels don't tell us anything about what the growing-up years of Jesus and his brothers and sisters were like. We know he had brothers named James, Joseph, Simon, and Judas, and sisters who weren't named (Matt. 13:55–56). What must it have been like to grow up with a big brother who never disobeyed, who always did the right thing, and who could impress all the rabbis at the temple with his questions as well as his answers? In one sense, I can't imagine how they didn't believe he was divine. How could they not be drawn to a brother who always loved them and those around them perfectly? But then, any of us who grew up with siblings also recognize that it can be incredibly annoying, even alienating, to have a sibling whose good behavior is always making us look bad. I wonder if that was part of the reason that once Jesus transitioned out of the shop in Nazareth to miraculous ministry around Galilee, Jesus's brothers and sisters not only rejected him, they wanted to put him away.

Jesus was making his way around Galilee, calling demons to come out of a man, claiming to be Lord of the Sabbath, cleansing a leper, declaring a paralytic's sins to be forgiven. Mark records, "Then he went home, and the crowd gathered again, so that they could not even eat. And when his family heard it, they went out to seize him, for they were saying, 'He is out of his mind'" (Mark 3:20–21).

This was embarrassing. Did Jesus not realize he was making the whole family look ridiculous by claiming the authority of God to do such things? Mark continues:

> And his mother and his brothers came, and standing outside they sent to him and called him. And a crowd was sitting around him, and they said to him, "Your mother and your brothers are outside, seeking you." And he answered them, "Who are my mother and my brothers?" And looking about

at those who sat around him, he said, "Here are my mother and my brothers! For whoever does the will of God, he is my brother and sister and mother." (Mark 3:31–35)

Jesus used the opportunity to reveal something very significant about the human family as well as what it means to be a part of his family. Human family is important, but it isn't everything. According to Jesus, there is a family that takes precedence over our biological families—and that is the family made up of our spiritual mothers and fathers, brothers and sisters, the family made up of all who are related by faith and obedience to Jesus.

Notice that Jesus said that his family are those who do the will of God. So the way to be related to him is not through biology but through obedience. Once again, as we observed in the lives of Joseph and Mary, we're hearing the refrain of hearing and obeying God's word as the key to being in God's family. In fact, Jesus stated it clearly at one point. Jesus was teaching in a way that was unlike any teaching the people had heard before when "a woman in the crowd raised her voice and said to him, 'Blessed is the womb that bore you, and the breasts at which you nursed!' But he said, 'Blessed rather are those who hear the word of God and keep it!'" (Luke 11:27–28).

There is a greater blessedness than being related to Jesus by blood. This greater satisfaction and blessedness is available to anyone, no matter what your ancestry, no matter what kind of family you were born into. Even now, you are hearing the word of God. Seek to make it part of the fabric of your life. Keep the word of God by doing what it tells you to do. Find all your hope and security and identity, not in your human family, but in Jesus.

We gain another insight into Jesus's siblings in the Gospel of John. Jesus had just fed five thousand people with five barley loaves and two fish. All was well and good until Jesus explained what he had intended to communicate through this miracle: "Truly, truly, I say to you, unless you eat the flesh of the Son of

Man and drink his blood, you have no life in you" (John 6:53). Eat his flesh and drink his blood? What did he mean by that? Many who heard his words were offended by the very idea. The chapter ends with the report that "many of his disciples turned back and no longer walked with him." Then John 7 opens:

> After this Jesus went about in Galilee. He would not go about in Judea, because the Jews were seeking to kill him. Now the Jews' Feast of Booths was at hand. So his brothers said to him, "Leave here and go to Judea, that your disciples also may see the works you are doing. For no one works in secret if he seeks to be known openly. If you do these things, show yourself to the world." For not even his brothers believed in him. (John 7:1–5)

Is that not a terribly sad sentence? "For not even his brothers believed in him." Their lack of belief was not, however, a hindrance to their desire to ride his coattails if he was gaining in popularity. It didn't keep them from giving Jesus what seemed to them to be good advice. The Feast of Booths (or Tabernacles) drew thousands to Jerusalem, and if Jesus went there and performed some miracles, they thought it would be a big boost to his notoriety. Jesus's brothers wanted Jesus to put on a display of miracles for the largest audience possible.

Indeed, Jesus did intend to put himself on display in Jerusalem but not in the way his brothers thought. Jesus would put himself on display in Jerusalem by being hung on a Roman cross. Indeed, when he was lifted up from the earth, he would draw all people to himself (John 12:32).

Amazingly, among those Jesus would draw to himself were his slow-to-believe brothers and sisters. They were not there at his crucifixion. To have a brother sentenced to die such a hideous death was the ultimate embarrassment and shame. Jesus's mother was there alone, so Jesus appointed the apostle John to care for her.

But then something happened that changed everything. We read in 1 Corinthians 15:7 that after Jesus was raised from the dead, he appeared "to James, then to all the apostles." This James was Jesus's brother James. In grace, the risen, glorified Jesus revealed himself to one of his brothers who had heretofore refused to believe in him. In fact, Jesus's brother James not only became a believer but the leader of the church in Jerusalem. James, the half brother of Jesus, wrote the book of James in the Bible, which, interestingly, focuses on not only hearing the word of God but also living it out. Another half brother, Jude, wrote the book by his name.

What I find most interesting about these two brothers of Jesus is the way they introduced themselves at the beginning of their letters. If it were me, I would likely want to start my letter like this: "Nancy, half sister of Jesus [you know, someone who grew up with him and knew him longer and better than most people]." But James and Jude didn't even mention their sibling relationship in their books. They defined themselves, not as half brothers of Jesus, but as servants of Jesus. James began his letter, "James, a servant of God and of the Lord Jesus Christ" (James 1:1). And Jude began his brief letter, "Jude, a servant of Jesus Christ and brother of James" (Jude 1).

James and Jude clearly came to see Jesus not merely as sibling but as Savior. And not just the Savior of the world out there, but *their* Savior, the *only* Savior. They went from wanting to silence Jesus to giving their lives to serve Jesus. Rather than being embarrassed by him, they gloried in calling him Lord. James wrote, "There is only one lawgiver and judge, he who is able to save and to destroy" (James 4:12). And Jude wrote that it is only Jesus who "is able to keep you from stumbling and to present you blameless before the presence of his glory with great joy" (Jude 24).

Perhaps there is some encouragement in the story of Jesus's siblings for those of us who have family members who have, so far, rejected Jesus. These siblings of Jesus spent their whole lives living with and working beside one who lived his life perfectly and communicated God's word perfectly. So if you are brokenhearted by unbelief in a loved one's life, and you're beating yourself up thinking that if only you'd been a better witness, a better example, or if you could only explain things better, then your loved one would embrace Christ—you can stop pointing the finger of blame toward yourself. Don't give up praying. And don't take their resistance as the final word. Look at Jesus's family and see:

The family of Jesus is made up of people whose belief is better-late-than-never.

Maybe someone in your family has been slow to believe. Or perhaps you are the one who has been slow to believe, slow to confess that you have been wrong about Jesus up to this point, slow to commit to a new way of living. At this point, perhaps you think it would just be too embarrassing and too humbling to admit that you've been wrong, that you've been missing something, that really, you've been outside the family of genuine faith when perhaps everyone who knows you assumes otherwise.

It's not too late. The family of Jesus is made up of people whose belief is better-late-than-never. If James could spend decades around Jesus without believing in him and then have his life completely changed by him, so can you. If Jude could go from being resistant to Jesus's authority to cherishing Jesus's authority in his life, so can you.

The family of Jesus is made up of sinners who found grace and forgiveness in him. It is made up of those who have some understanding of who Jesus is but are seeking more, those who have heard God's word and want to spend the rest of their lives seeking to obey it, and those who have waited and resisted and refused to believe in Jesus and now want to call him Lord and Master.

So I have to ask: Do you see any of these family traits in your own life?

Do you have a less-than-perfect record? If so, are you willing to accept that Jesus took your less-than-perfect record upon himself on the cross and that he stands offering to you his own perfect record in its place? Will you receive grace?

Do you understand some things about Jesus but still have so much you don't understand? Don't think you have to have everything figured out before you come to him. As you turn to him with your limited amount of understanding, he will fill you with his Spirit, who will work in you so that your understanding of Jesus will grow.

Does it just seem too embarrassing to you to admit, perhaps having grown up in or having spent a long time in church circles, that you've never really crossed the line into genuine repentance and faith, never gone from being a spiritually dead person to a spiritually alive person?

Your brother, Jesus, wants to welcome you into his family. He wants to share with you all that he stands to inherit.

My husband, David, was actually able to trace his family line further back than Henry Guthrie, signer of the Cumberland Compact. He traced it back to John Guthrie, who left Angus, Scotland, with his parents, Captain James Montrose Guthrie and Elizabeth Guthrie, for the New World in the 1660s. Now maybe Angus, Scotland, means nothing to you, but Angus, Scotland, is where you find Guthrie Castle, built by Sir David Guthrie in 1468. I don't suppose the Guthries there were actually royalty, though evidently they did (at one time at least) live in a castle!

But David's sister recently took an expensive Uber ride to Guthrie Castle during a trip to Scotland, only to find it is now owned by an American and is no longer open to visitors. Not even Guthries.

This makes me so grateful to be part of another family, a greater family, a royal family. I've been adopted into the family that God promised Abraham he would bless and make a blessing. Paul writes, "For in Christ Jesus you are all sons of God, through faith. . . . And if you are Christ's, then you are Abraham's offspring, heirs according to promise" (Gal. 3:26, 29). In fact, I stand to inherit far more than an old castle in Scotland. I'm getting in on the promise to Abraham and his offspring that he would be heir of the world (Rom. 4:13). Jesus, my brother, has been appointed as heir of all things (Heb. 12:2), and he intends to share his inheritance with everyone who is a part of his family.

> Marvelous, infinite, matchless grace,
> Freely bestowed on all who believe;
> You that are longing to see his face,
> Will you this moment his grace receive?
>
> Grace, grace, God's grace,
> Grace that will pardon and cleanse within;
> Grace, grace, God's grace,
> Grace that is greater than all our sin.[6]

3

THE ROCK

Have you ever run into someone you haven't seen for years that you didn't recognize because his or her appearance had changed so much? David and I are at the age that when we see people we haven't seen for a long time we sometimes think, *Wow, they've gotten old!* And then we cringe at the reality that they probably think the same thing about us.

Of course, these are just external changes. What is really amazing (and perhaps more rare) is to be around someone who has significantly changed in far more profound and personal ways—someone who used to be impatient, difficult to please, or easily angered, but is now softer, kinder, and more patient. Perhaps you see someone who always used to need to be in charge and have things revolve around her, now serving quietly in the shadows. She's become genuinely more concerned about the needs and concerns of others than her own.

That's the kind of change we're really interested in. So how does that kind of change happen? And can it really last?

When it comes to change, I think for most of us, there is a resistance (we're comfortable with things the way they are, thank you very much) as well as a fear that we can never change (we've tried and failed, and the fear of wanting to change and discovering that we can't is embarrassing and immobilizing). Most of us know what it's like to determine that we are going to change something about ourselves or our lives—change our diets, our sleep, our exercise routines, or the way we interact with particular difficult people or situations. Maybe we succeed for a while, but few of us are able to change in ways that stick, ways that become an intrinsic part of who we are.

Recently my son was cleaning out a closet and found a picture of his fifth-grade football team. All those guys were eleven or twelve years old in the picture and are now in their late twenties. As we looked at the individual faces, we talked about how the basic personality traits, inclinations, and interests of most of those guys have pretty much stayed the same as when they were in elementary school. So much about who we are seems hard-wired into us, doesn't it?

That makes us wonder: *Is it really possible to change?* Is it realistic to think that we could ever change from being naturally cynical into people who instinctively assume the best of others? Could we change from being people who naturally tend toward self-preservation, self-focus, and selfishness into people who give and defer to others in costly ways? Is it possible we could ever change from being naturally fearful people into people who face the future with confidence and courage?

Perhaps you wonder about yourself:

+ Will I always be so defensive, or could I become open to careful criticism?
+ Will I ever be able to resist entertaining lustful thoughts and sexual fantasies, or will I always be easily drawn into indulging them?
+ Will I ever develop an internal desire to read and study the Bible, or is it always going to be a battle of the will?
+ Will my first instinct always be to navigate and manipulate myself into getting the best, being the first, and having

the most, or will there come a day when I will genuinely be able to rejoice at what other people have, get to do and enjoy, even if I don't?

In the story of Jesus, we get an up-close, personal view of a number of people's transformations, but perhaps none is as significant as Simon Peter's. Between the Simon we encounter in the stories found in the Gospels and the Peter we encounter in his preaching and writing in Acts and his two epistles, it is as if Simon Peter has been on one of those makeover television shows! The main difference being that his is not an external makeover; it's an internal one. There are ways in which we hardly recognize him to be the same person. But seeing that he is, in fact, the same person gives us hope! Comparing the before and after pictures of Simon Peter gives us hope that the same Savior—the same Spirit who brought genuine, lasting change in Simon Peter—could work to bring about genuine, lasting change in us too.

Real Change Begins with Jesus's Call

Our first glimpse of Simon comes in John 1, when he was introduced to Jesus. Andrew, Simon's brother, was one of the many who had been captivated by the voice—the voice of John the Baptist crying in the wilderness. Andrew was there at the Jordan when John the Baptist pointed toward Jesus and said, "Behold, the Lamb of God," and he could hardly wait to tell his brother about Jesus. John records, "He first found his own brother Simon and said to him, 'We have found the Messiah' (which means Christ)" (John 1:41).

Andrew was exactly right that Jesus was the Messiah, the anointed one, the Christ, but he certainly said far more than he fully understood at that point. It became clear that he and all the other disciples had a great deal to learn about the Messiah and his mission—their understanding was limited and, at times, distorted.

John writes that when Andrew brought his brother Simon to Jesus, "Jesus looked at him and said, 'You are Simon the son of John. You shall be called Cephas' (which means Peter)" (John 1:42). Today, we might say it like this: "You are Simon Johnson, but there is going to come a day when that name won't fit you anymore. Your identity won't rest on your connection to your earthy father. You'll be Peter (which means Rock)." Usually when someone gives a person a name—a nickname—it has to do with some past event or some current reality about them. But this was clearly different. This name reflected who or what Simon would become—a rock, a stone. He was currently impulsive, ambitious, outspoken Simon Johnson, but grace was going to go to work in him, and he would become someone very different.

Jesus told Peter who he would become by becoming joined to him. But this wouldn't happen instantly or painlessly. In fact, it would include failure; it would be messy, embarrassing, stumbling, humbling, and costly. It would be a miracle—but a miracle accomplished over the course of Peter's lifetime, not in an instant.

It was not that Jesus saw rock-like potential in Simon to develop. Simon was far from a rock at this point. This new name (which even Jesus would not use for quite some time) was a reflection of what Jesus intended to accomplish in and through Peter by grace. Indeed, this is always the way sinners are transformed into saints. God "calls into existence the things that do not exist" (Rom. 4:17).

You see, when Jesus told Peter he would be a rock, it was the Rock, the stumbling stone, the Cornerstone, looking into the face of Simon, whom the Father had chosen and predestined before the foundations of the world to be conformed to the image of his Son. Peter's "rock-ness" (and yes, I realize I have just made up a word) would be derived from his connection to the Rock. Peter did not decide he wanted to become a more reliable, more solid, better, wiser leader and simply will himself into that transformation.

This was a transformation that was a work of grace, start to finish, by the one who was about to call Simon Peter to himself.

Some time after this initial meeting when, "the crowd was pressing in on [Jesus] to hear the word of God, he was standing by the lake of Gennesaret, and he saw two boats by the lake, but the fishermen had gone out of them and were washing their nets" (Luke 5:1–2). Andrew and Simon Peter were methodically maintaining the tools of their trade, the nets they used to catch fish. Except, on this day, they really hadn't caught many fish.

And then Jesus approached them. "Getting into one of the boats, which was Simon's, [Jesus] asked him to put out a little from the land. And he sat down and taught the people from the boat" (Luke 5:3). Peter pushed out a bit from the shoreline that was filled with his friends and neighbors. They were all listening to Jesus talk about life and God and his kingdom in a way they'd never heard before from their religious leaders. "And when he had finished speaking, [Jesus] said to Simon, 'Put out into the deep and let down your nets for a catch'" (v. 4).

Simon Peter had fished these waters since he was a boy in his father's boat. He knew the habits of the fish, as well as the best timing, location, and conditions for taking in a haul of fish. Jesus had spent all his life as a craftsman working with tools (not as a fisherman working with nets), yet here he was, telling Simon to let down his nets.

> And Simon answered, "Master, we toiled all night and took nothing! But at your word I will let down the nets." And when they had done this, they enclosed a large number of fish, and their nets were breaking. They signaled to their partners in the other boat to come and help them. And they came and filled both the boats. (Luke 5:5–7)

What Simon Peter could not know was that a divine call had gone out to the shoals of fish, filling them with an irresistible impulse to swim toward his nets. He also did not know that an equally irresistible divine call had gone out for him. "And Jesus said to Simon, 'Do not be afraid; from now on you will be catching men.' And when they had brought their boats to land, they left everything and followed him" (Luke 5:10–11).

The day would come, on Pentecost, when Peter would let down his net in Jerusalem, and this miracle would be repeated but in a whole new way. Three thousand souls would hear and respond to the irresistible call of Jesus and come into the safety of his net. Still later, Peter would once again let down his net in the Gentile household of a Roman centurion named Cornelius. Peter would tell of the life, death, and resurrection of Jesus, and the Holy Spirit would fall on all who heard the word (Acts 10:44). By the power of the Holy Spirit, they would be swept into the net.[7]

This is the way real change begins in our lives. Real change does not begin with our initiative, our sense of a need to improve ourselves, or our decision to work our way through programs of personal transformation. Real, lasting change that transforms us into the people God has created us to be begins with God taking the initiative in our lives. He is the one who foreknew you, chose you, called you, and predestined you to be conformed to the image of his Son.

Real Change Requires Divine Revelation

The second thing Simon Peter showed us about real and lasting change is that it doesn't come because we figure something out or because someone provides us with insight or a successful strategy. Instead, it comes as a result of divine revelation. Maybe that sounds strange or uncomfortable to you because you have assumed that your life will change based on whether or not you are able to figure things out. But the reality is, unless the Father chooses to reveal to us who Jesus really is, all our efforts to change will be limited by human ideas and human power.

From the time Simon left his nets, his home, his family, and his old identity to follow Jesus, he had a front-row seat to discover who Jesus really was. He saw Jesus heal those who came with all kinds of diseases, including Simon's own mother-in-law. Simon took part in the miracle of loaves and fishes being multiplied so that more than five thousand people gathered on a hillside were fed. He heard Jesus teach with a kind of authority that he'd never witnessed before. Simon stepped out of the boat in the middle of a storm, believing that he could walk on water to Jesus. He regularly saw Jesus slip away to commune with his Father in prayer. He had a front-row seat to see who Jesus was.

He and the rest of the disciples had been with Jesus for about eighteen months and had, perhaps, settled into seeing him as a great teacher and wonder-worker. But this understanding of Jesus simply didn't have the power to create any significant and lasting change in their lives. So Jesus pressed the point with them.

> Now when Jesus came into the district of Caesarea Philippi, he asked his disciples, "Who do people say that the Son of Man is?" And they said, "Some say John the Baptist, others say Elijah, and others Jeremiah or one of the prophets." (Matt. 16:13–14)

The disciples told Jesus that the people around them thought he was a prophet. So much of what Jesus said and did reminded them of the Old Testament prophets. In a sense, they were right. Jesus was the prophet par excellence, but he was and is much more than a prophet. These people who thought he was one of the prophets didn't quite have the whole picture. So Jesus posed the question much more personally: "'But who do you say that I am?' And Simon Peter replied, 'You are the Christ, the Son of the living God'" (Matt. 16:15–16).

Simon spoke up for the group, as he had a habit of doing, making clear that they were coming to recognize that Jesus was not only prophet but also priest and king. "The Christ" indicated he was the anointed one. He was the one all the kings and priests who were anointed with oil throughout the centuries had pointed toward. Jesus was not just the son of Mary and Joseph; he was the Son of the living God.

> And Jesus answered him, "Blessed are you, Simon Bar-Jonah! For flesh and blood has not revealed this to you, but my Father who is in heaven." (Matt. 16:17)

Simon and the rest had not figured this out through their own ability to observe and evaluate data. Something supernatural had happened among them. They had experienced a divine revelation so that they now had a truly supernatural and transformational understanding of who Jesus was. This is the kind of solid foundation a person could build a life on.

Jesus continued, "And I tell you, you are Peter, and on this rock I will build my church, and the gates of hell shall not prevail against it" (Matt. 16:18). "You are Peter." Clearly, the change that Jesus foresaw in Simon's life when they first met was coming about. There was a new solidity to Simon's grasp of the identity of Jesus, a divine wisdom replacing his natural foolishness. Jesus is, according to the Scriptures, the rock of refuge, the rock of our salvation, the rock who was struck so that living water flowed out, the stone the builders rejected that has become the cornerstone, a stone of offense and a rock of stumbling. Jesus, the Rock, looked at Peter (who was becoming a chip off the old Rock) and the rest of the disciples and said that a foundation was being built through their growing grasp of who he was. On this foundation of recognizing Jesus as the Christ, the church would be built. This spiritual house, as Peter would later refer to it in his letter, would have such a solid cornerstone in Jesus and such a solid foundation in the gospel of Jesus proclaimed by these apostles, it would prove to be invincible even when the armies of hell do their best to destroy it. The testimony of the twelve would be fashioned into the foundation stones of a new humanity. The message of the gospel that they were going to proclaim would open the doors to the kingdom of heaven for those who heard and believed.

What we see happening in Peter and the other disciples is what we want to see happen in our own lives. We want an increasing clarity, surety, and stability. So how does this happen? Ultimately it doesn't come as a result of our own curiosity or even our own desperation to find something real and true. It comes through divine revelation. The only people who ever come to discover and truly experience God in his fullness are those to whom he chooses to reveal himself. This included Peter and the rest of the disciples, and this includes you and me.

This means that if you have come to know and love Jesus, the Christ, it is not because of anything special in you. We want to think that we were spiritually sensitive enough, smart enough, sincere enough to choose Jesus. But in reality, if you are alive in Christ, it is only because of a work of grace emanating out of the heart of God toward a spiritually dead sinner. And if you are not yet quite sure about Jesus, perhaps hovering around but not yet joined to Jesus by faith, this means that the most important prayer you can pray is to ask God to reveal to you who Jesus really is and what he is really worth in an unmistakable, unavoidable, life-giving, life-altering way.

Real Change Is Tested by Various Trials

Peter must have been on an emotional high after Jesus affirmed his confession that Jesus was the Christ. So the next interaction between Jesus and Simon Peter recorded by Matthew must have been crushing. Matthew writes:

> From that time Jesus began to show his disciples that he must go to Jerusalem and suffer many things from the elders and chief priests and scribes, and be killed, and on the third day be raised. And Peter took him aside and began to rebuke him, saying, "Far be it from you, Lord! This shall never happen to you." But he turned and said to Peter, "Get behind me, Satan! You are a hindrance to me. For you are not setting your

63

mind on the things of God, but on the things of man." (Matt. 16:21–23)

One minute Simon Peter articulated what could only have been revealed to him by God, and the next minute his words were distinctly human. One minute Jesus told him he was going to be used to build the church, and the next minute that he was being used by Satan to hinder Jesus's ransom of the church. One minute he seemed to understand what the Christ had come into the world to accomplish, and the next minute he seemed to have no sense of how Christ's saving work would be accomplished.

At this point, Simon Peter had no interest in Christ being crucified; he wanted Christ to conquer. He wanted Jesus to march into Jerusalem to engage in holy war. Of course, Jesus would enter into battle in Jerusalem. But he would be crushed in that battle, put to death in that battle. Rather than being crowned as king, he would be mocked as king. Rather than being lifted up to a glorious throne, he would be lifted up on a shameful cross.

Jesus, however, was not done responding to Peter's rebuke. Jesus went on to say that not only was there a cross in his own future, but the cross would be a reality in the lives of anyone and everyone who wanted to be his disciple. "Then Jesus told his disciples, 'If anyone would come after me, let him deny himself and take up his cross and follow me. For whoever would save his life will lose it, but whoever loses his life for my sake will find it'" (Matt. 16:24–25).

I think most of us would have to admit that when we hear that following Jesus is going to require that we take up his cross, we hesitate. We were looking for self-improvement, not self-denial. Yes, we want to be like Jesus, but we don't really want to suffer like Jesus or to suffer for Jesus. We were hoping to use this thing called prayer to pray away suffering, not to pray for perseverance in suffering.

Clearly that was the case for Simon Peter and for the rest of Jesus's disciples. They were right there with Jesus in the comfort of the upper room and the closeness of the garden . . . until a mob showed up to arrest Jesus. I think some of the saddest words in the Bible are: "Then all the disciples left him and fled" (Matt. 26:56). There in the garden, Simon Peter had been so self-confident: "Though they all fall away because of you, I will never fall away" he had said (Matt. 26:33). But minutes later, he was fleeing in fear. Later that night, he would swear, "I do not know the man" (Matt. 26:72, 74). Clearly, his recognition of Jesus and a desire to be with Jesus wasn't enough. When put to the test of suffering for Jesus, he was still the same old Simon.

But between the Simon we see in this scene and the Peter we meet in the opening chapters of Acts, something clearly changed. As the story progresses in Acts, we find Peter regularly submitted to suffering for Jesus's sake. He is beaten and imprisoned because he just will not stop talking about King Jesus.

So how did this change come about in Peter? I want to know, don't you? I want to experience this kind of transformation in my own life. I want to be changed into a woman who has such rock-solid confidence in who Jesus is, what he has accomplished for me, and what he's preparing for me, that even when it begins to cost me something, I will not flee, deny, or drift from him.

Perhaps we find an answer to that question in Peter's letter that he wrote many years later to believers who were scattered in various parts of the known world. Rather than read these verses as he wrote them to his readers, I hope you'll allow me to adapt them slightly to turn them into Peter's personal testimony of how this change came about in his life. Hear Peter saying:

> Blessed be the God and Father of my Lord Jesus Christ! According to his great mercy, he caused me to be born again to a living hope through the resurrection of Jesus Christ from the dead, to an inheritance that is imperishable, undefiled, and unfading, kept in heaven for me. By God's power, I am being guarded through faith for a salvation ready to be revealed in the last time. In this I rejoice, though now for a little while, if necessary, I have been grieved by various trials, so that the

tested genuineness of my faith—more precious than gold that perishes though it is tested by fire—may be found to result in praise and glory and honor at the revelation of Jesus Christ. (adapted from 1 Pet. 1:3–7)

Change came about as the Holy Spirit applied the power of the life, death, and resurrection of Jesus to Peter's life. Think about what this means. As Peter was joined to Jesus Christ through faith, the power that enabled Jesus to face the humiliation of the cross began to flow into Peter, providing him the power to face the humiliations of persecution. As Peter was joined to Jesus Christ through faith, the power that raised Jesus from the dead began to flow into Peter's life, so that new life began to sprout in the dead places of his life and character. He had fresh courage in place of the old fears. He had a new God-confidence in place of his old self-confidence. Godly wisdom supplanted Peter's naturally foolish impulses. As the Holy Spirit applied the power of Christ's death and resurrection to Peter's life, Peter had the power he needed to deny himself and take up his cross.

And for Peter, that cross was not at all symbolic or spiritualized. It was real. When Jesus served breakfast to Peter on the seashore following Christ's resurrection, the risen Savior told Peter that the day would come when he would stretch out his hands in death. And while it is not recorded in the Bible, historians tell us that Peter died by crucifixion. Not wanting to die in the same way as his Savior, Peter, by then an old man, asked to be crucified upside down.

Simon was transformed into Peter, the Rock. The change began as the Holy Spirit united Simon Peter to Christ in Christ's life, death, and resurrection. And it continued progressively over the course of a lifetime as that power worked its way through Peter's natural personality and inclinations. And here's the good news for you and me: the Spirit who applied the power of the death and resurrection to Peter is the same Spirit who seals you and me to Christ so that that same power flows into us!

My friend, it is not up to you to work up the power to change the things in your life you want to change. As you become joined to Christ by faith and feed on Christ by reading his word, hearing it preached, meditating on it, ingesting the sacraments week by week, and as you abide in Christ and among his people, the Holy Spirit goes to work changing the things in you that he wants to change. And that is key—it is the change he intends, not necessarily what you identify and desire to be changed. You can expect that there will be some friction as he goes to work. Some of what he intends to change about you is going to rub you the wrong way. And you can be sure that the genuineness of that change will be tested through suffering.

But, if you are genuinely joined to Christ, it will really happen. And it will become evident, not just to you, but to those around you too, by how you respond to the ordinary challenges of life—being delayed, disappointed, inconvenienced, interrupted, insulted, overlooked, or underappreciated. It will be even more evident when you face devastating loss, overwhelming pain, and unjust treatment. This is when you and I get the opportunity to live out genuine faith that "[will] result in praise and glory and honor at the revelation of Jesus Christ" (1 Pet. 1:7). The change in us, empowered by him, will result in his receiving praise and glory and honor when he comes again.

Oh, my friend, won't that be a great day, when Christ's transforming work in us to change us—from being cold to kind, greedy to generous, impulsive to self-controlled, anxious to restful—results in Jesus Christ being given praise and glory for all the world to see?

Real Change Is Granted by Divine Power

The reason Jesus will receive praise and glory for the change in you and me is that he is the one granting us the power to change. We're not working it up ourselves. Peter understood this about himself and about every person who is in Christ. That was why he could write the following words in 2 Peter 1. But, once again, allow me to adjust it slightly into the form of Peter's testimony about his own experience. Hear Peter testifying:

> His divine power has granted to me all things that pertain to life and godliness, through the knowledge of him who called me to his own glory and excellence, by which he has granted to me his precious and very great promises, so that through them I have become a partaker of the divine nature, having escaped from the corruption that is in the world because of sinful desire. (adapted from 2 Pet. 1:3–5)

This was Peter's personal experience: divine power granted to him so that he was no longer driven by sinful desires for worldly significance or worldly power. Instead, the divine power of Jesus flowed into his life, creating real, lasting, ongoing, pervasive change.

That is not just the way it happened for Peter. That's the way it happens for any and all of us. If my life is going to be transformed from what I am by nature to what I'm called to be by grace, Jesus alone can do it.

+ The only way I can live by faith is if Jesus gives that faith to me.
+ The only way I can keep from failing is if Jesus prays for me.
+ The only way I can recognize who Jesus is, is if the Spirit reveals it to me.
+ The only way I can speak up with courage in the face of persecution and suffering is if the Spirit provides that courage to me.
+ The only way I can serve others in humility is if the humility of Jesus flows through me.

Imagine seeing someone you haven't seen for a while, and she says to you, "You know, you've changed. You're different." And imagine being able to say in response, "Let me tell you what has happened. I have become a partaker of the divine nature."

Real change—the kind that turns a Simon into a Peter or a scoundrel into a saint—is not apprehended through good intentions, personal grit, rigorous accountability, or a decision of the will. It flows into our lives as we are joined to Jesus Christ. The Holy Spirit applies the death and resurrection power of Jesus Christ to the areas of our lives that are resistant to change. The Holy Spirit applies this power to the places in our minds and bodies and spirits where we are dead to God and alive to our own desires, inclinations, and orientations. We find that we have a new power to say "no" to those desires that is not a power we developed on our own. It has been granted to us. We become living, breathing, walking, talking miracles of grace.

That's what Peter was.

+ In the Gospels, we read that when Simon's nets were filled with more fish than he could load into his boat, his first response was to fall down at Jesus's knees, saying, "Depart from me, for I am a sinful man, O Lord" (Luke 5:8). But everything changed for him with the cross and resurrection so that Peter could write in his first letter, "He himself bore our sins in his body on the tree, that we might die to sin and live to righteousness" (1 Pet. 2:24). The way he saw himself, his sin, and his life had completely changed.

+ In the Gospels, we hear Simon rebuke Jesus for suggesting he was going to suffer. In his epistle, we read the words of Peter, a man who had been in the fire, telling us not to be surprised at the fiery trial when it comes to test us, as though something strange were happening to us. He says, "Rejoice insofar as you share Christ's sufferings, that you may also rejoice and be glad when his glory is revealed" (1 Pet. 4:12–13). Peter was changed. He found his happiness in a very different way than he did before.

+ In the Gospels, we see that Simon was among the twelve who had no interest in washing anyone else's feet. Then, when Jesus took up the towel to wash Simon's feet, he told

Jesus, "You shall never wash my feet," demonstrating that he had no understanding of how a life of serving others flows out of being served by Jesus. But in his letter, all resistance to serving others is gone. Peter wrote that we should each use whatever gift we have been given to serve one another, not so that others will be impressed with our service, but "in order that in everything God may be glorified through Jesus Christ" (1 Pet. 4:11).

✦ In the Gospels, Jesus told Simon that Satan had asked to sift him like wheat. Indeed, Simon would be shaken to the core by the crucifixion of Jesus and his own denials of Jesus. But Jesus's prayer for Simon, that he would become a source of strength to his brothers, became a reality. In Acts, we see Peter declare Jesus rather than deny him. He's become rock-like. When he was sifted, his faith did not ultimately fail.

Do you long for change? Me too. The good news of the gospel is that who we are by nature can be transformed by grace. If you are in Christ, if you are partaking of the ordinary means by which his grace and power are delivered to us—the preaching and reading of God's word, fellowship with other believers, talking to God through prayer, participation in the sacraments of baptism and the Lord's Supper—you can be confident that the Holy Spirit is using those means to create organic change in your character, your desires, your thoughts, your values, and your perspective.

You can also be sure that the Holy Spirit will fill you with a bit of holy discontentment in regard to how much change has taken place in your life until the day you die because even on that day, he will still not be done changing you. A day of ultimate change will still be coming. "Behold! I tell you a mystery," wrote Paul, "for the trumpet will sound, and the dead will be raised imperishable, and we shall be changed" (1 Cor. 15:51–52).

Jesus will come and call us. On that day, the tested genuineness of our faith will result in praise and glory and honor as Jesus Christ

is revealed. He who began a good work in us will have brought it
to completion at the day of Jesus Christ.

> My hope is built on nothing less
> Than Jesus' blood and righteousness;
> I dare not trust the sweetest frame,
> But wholly lean on Jesus' name.
>
> On Christ, the solid Rock, I stand;
> All other ground is sinking sand,
> All other ground is sinking sand.[8]

4

THE HYPOCRITES

"When I grow up, I want to be . . . a hypocrite" said no one ever. Hypocrisy is the antithesis of sincerity and the opposite of integrity. Nobody sets out to be a person who says one thing and does another or a person who puts on a false face to the world. Certainly no one ever sets out to become the very worst kind of hypocrite—a religious hypocrite. So how does it happen? If a person does become a religious hypocrite, does she know it, or is hypocrisy something that we hide even from ourselves—something so uncomfortable, and yet so comfortable, we could be blissfully unaware of it?

Is there some test we can take or some mirror we can look into that would reveal any hypocrisy in our lives that needs to be dealt the deathblow of honesty and humility? You know, like the tests comedian Jeff Foxworthy provides for anyone who wants to figure out if he or she is a redneck? Like, "If you've ever cut your grass and found a car, you might be a redneck," or "If you've got a complete set of salad bowls and every one of them says 'Cool Whip,' you might be a redneck." [9]

We may not be concerned about whether or not we're rednecks, but we do want to do some self-examination to discover if we might be hypocritical when it comes to our connectedness to Christ. So, with apologies to Jeff Foxworthy, let me try a few . . .

+ If you've ever said, "I'll pray for you," and didn't actually pray, you might be a religious hypocrite.
+ If you've ever said, "I forgive you," but continued telling others how you'd been wronged, you might be a religious hypocrite.
+ If you've ever said, "Amen," to someone's prayer, even though you'd actually been making a mental grocery list during the prayer, you might be a religious hypocrite.
+ If your lips have uttered the words, "Your kingdom come, your will be done," while having no intention of submitting to God in a particular area of your life, you might be a religious hypocrite.
+ If you regularly watch explicit programs that you'd never watch with church friends, lest they think you are not as holy as you want to appear, you might be a religious hypocrite.
+ If your words to your family on the way to church are often harsh or unkind, but then you're friendly to everyone at church, you might be a religious hypocrite.
+ If you've ever been glad to be observed donating money to your church, a mission project, or a "Go Fund Me" page for a particular cause, you might be a religious hypocrite.
+ If you have judged others for their judgmental attitudes and actions, you might be a religious hypocrite.
+ If you've ever hoped people would think that you're reading the Bible on your phone during church when in reality you were scrolling through social media, you might be a religious hypocrite.
+ If you've ever used phrases like "the Lord led us" or "God told me" simply to make your choice sound more spiritual, you might be a religious hypocrite.
+ If you've ever posted something on social media hoping that viewers will think you are more virtuous, more com-

passionate, more "woke," or more "with it," than you really are, you might be a religious hypocrite.

I know. Nailed. *Ouch*.

We really don't want to be religious hypocrites. We want to be people who are authentic, people of integrity, people whose lives are consistent with what we say we believe. So let's spend a little time looking at those whom Jesus—who recognizes sincerity as well as hypocrisy—called out for their religious hypocrisy.

We're going to hop, skip, and jump a bit through the book of Matthew to peek into Jesus's interactions with, and statements about, the most notorious religious hypocrites in his day—the scribes and Pharisees. Then we'll land in Matthew 23 and listen in on Jesus's bold, straightforward, brokenhearted pronouncement of the disaster that was ahead for these scoundrels.

Who Were the Pharisees?

The first time the scribes and the Pharisees show up in Matthew's Gospel is Matthew 5:20, in what we call the Sermon on the Mount. As he spoke on a hillside in Galilee, Jesus described what was required to be a citizen of his kingdom, a member of his family, a partaker in all of what it means to belong to him. In this sermon he said, "For I tell you, unless your righteousness exceeds that of the scribes and Pharisees, you will never enter the kingdom of heaven" (Matt. 5:20). It is probably hard for that statement to hit us the same way it had to have hit those who were listening to him on the hillside that day. Most of us have a mental image of the Pharisees that is a cross between a member of the Taliban and Snidely Whiplash, from the Rocky and Bullwinkle cartoons, with his villainous black mustache. The word "Pharisee" conjures up the image of judgmental, conniving, and even murderous men. But, if you and I lived in the time of Jesus, we would not have seen the Pharisees as evil; we would have honored them as heroes.

We have to review a bit of history to understand who the Pharisees were and what made them who they were. If we shift back to Old Testament history, we remember that the Babylonians carried off the people of Judah into exile. Then the Persians came into power, and Cyrus the Great allowed the Jews in exile to return to Judea to rebuild their temple. But there were decades between these events when there was no temple in Jerusalem, and Jews were scattered throughout the known world. It was during this era that synagogues began to be built in various towns and cities. In the synagogues, prayers were offered and the Torah (the books of God's law written by Moses) was read aloud, interpreted, and taught by scribes and sages who were later called rabbis. Then Alexander the Great conquered Persia, and later the Seleucid Empire seized control and initiated a program of Hellenization, which tried to force Jews to abandon their own laws and customs. The Pharisees emerged as leaders in the resistance, and many of them lost their lives in what was called the Maccabean revolt. They were considered heroes of the faith by most Jewish people.

The Pharisees, however, did more than simply resist the efforts to diminish a Jewish sense of identity through obedience to God's law as written by Moses; they also added to God's law as written by Moses. They took commands in Exodus and Leviticus that were intended only for priests and imposed them on all Jews. God's law prescribed that priests were supposed to go through a cleansing ritual before offering sacrifices at the temple. The Pharisees imposed these cleansing rituals on everyone. God's law called on God's people to honor the Sabbath by ceasing from their ordinary work. The Pharisees took this invitation to rest with God (meant to anticipate the eternal rest God promised to provide) and turned it into a detailed rulebook of what people could and could not do on the Sabbath. The law in Leviticus called for fasting on the Day of Atonement as a part of mourning over sin, but the Pharisees turned fasting into a regular requirement. In fact, they fasted twice a week and made sure they looked hungry and acted cranky so that everyone would take note of their self-denial.

Legalism always seeks to reduce God's law to a humanly doable standard, to something we can keep, while also arrogantly condemning those who don't. The Pharisees turned God's law into a rigorous system, a burden. But God's law had really always been about loving God and neighbor from the heart. It had always been about being holy as he is holy. It had always been about pointing toward our need for one who would keep the law perfectly in our place.

The Pharisees didn't hold a sacred office like the priests, and they weren't a professional body like the scribes. They were a party, a bit like a political party in which people share a certain approach to how things ought to be done in government and society. At the heart of the Pharisee party was a commitment to the strictest separation from anything that might cause ceremonial defilement. They were law keepers on steroids and were viewed as the guardians of righteousness and purity in Israel. So when Jesus said, "Unless your righteousness exceeds that of the scribes and Pharisees, you will never enter the kingdom of heaven," the people must have thought, *Well, then, I might as well give up. That's going to be impossible. The scribes and Pharisees are the most righteous people I know.* The Pharisees represented the gold standard of righteousness as they constantly held themselves up for all to judge themselves against.

The next appearance of the Pharisees in Matthew's Gospel is in chapter 9:

> And as Jesus reclined at table in the house, behold, many tax collectors and sinners came and were reclining with Jesus and his disciples. And when the Pharisees saw this, they said to his disciples, "Why does your teacher eat with tax collectors and sinners?" (Matt. 9:10–13)

Jesus's consorting with notorious "sinners" showed that he had little time for the Pharisaical rules of ceremonial purity, which would have dictated avoiding such people. Since the Pharisees cared more about ceremonial purity than people in need of a Savior, they were offended. The chapter continues with one offense after another. In verse 14, Jesus's disciples were not fasting. In verse 32, Jesus healed a demon-possessed man. Is there anything more ceremonially unclean than a man possessed by demons?

When we get to Matthew 12, we hit the mother lode of Jesus's offenses toward the Pharisaical way of relating to God. The Sabbath was the biggest source of heavy-handed rule keeping imposed by the Pharisees. Jesus simply had no regard for their rules that missed what was meant to be the center of the Sabbath—the heart of a God who invites his people into rest not a God who imposes empty burdens on his people. Jesus's hungry disciples were plucking heads of grain to snack on as they walked through a field on the Sabbath. These heads of grain were clearly the last straw. The religion of the Pharisees was on a full-out collision course with the gospel of Jesus Christ. We read, "But the Pharisees went out and conspired against him, how to destroy him" (Matt. 12:14).

Teaching in the temple in Jerusalem the week before the Passover, Jesus made it clear that he knew about their conspiracy to kill him:

> Hear another parable. There was a master of a house who planted a vineyard and put a fence around it and dug a winepress in it and built a tower and leased it to tenants, and went into another country. When the season for fruit drew near, he sent his servants to the tenants to get his fruit. And the tenants took his servants and beat one, killed another, and stoned another. Again he sent other servants, more than the first. And they did the same to them. Finally he sent his son to them, saying, "They will respect my son." But when the tenants saw the son, they said to themselves, "This is the heir. Come, let us kill him and have his inheritance." And

they took him and threw him out of the vineyard and killed him. When therefore the owner of the vineyard comes, what will he do to those tenants? They said to him, "He will put those wretches to a miserable death and let out the vineyard to other tenants who will give him the fruits in their seasons." (Matt. 21:33–41)

A vineyard—the people of God were often described as a vineyard in the Old Testament. "Beat one, killed another, and stoned another"—the treatment of the servants in this parable brought to mind what God's prophets had experienced throughout Old Testament history. "My son"—the one telling this parable was the very one on whom the heavens opened, and the voice of God was heard saying, "This is my beloved Son, with whom I am well pleased" (Matt 3:17).

When the chief priests and the Pharisees heard [Jesus's] parables, they perceived that he was speaking about them. And although they were seeking to arrest him, they feared the crowds, because they held him to be a prophet. (Matt. 21:45–46)

They recognized themselves and their plan in Jesus's story. They wanted to throw him out of the vineyard, and they fully intended to kill him. They were just looking for an opportunity.

One might think that with the atmosphere so charged with hostility, Jesus would let that be his last word to or about the Pharisees. But no. He saw how much the crowds of people in his day, and even his own disciples, admired and were influenced by the Pharisees. Jesus also knew that if people followed the Pharisees' heartless, rule-keeping religion, it would not lead them into the life they longed for. It would only bind them up and ultimately destroy them. So what did Jesus do?

There were crowds of pilgrims gathered at Jerusalem for the Passover. He was speaking to them about the scribes and the Pharisees. So he turned from the Pharisees to speak to "the crowds and to his disciples" (Matt. 23:1). He worked his way through a list of attitudes and actions of the Pharisees, revealing what was really at work in the hearts of those they revered and might have been tempted to not just admire but follow. As we consider what was at the heart of their religious hypocrisy, we want to check our own hearts and lives against the list. We want to use it as an opportunity to be honest with ourselves and with God and so escape any hypocritical tendencies in our lives.

What Was the Problem with the Pharisees?

1. Religious hypocrites are more interested in being an authority than in living under authority.

> The scribes and the Pharisees sit on Moses' seat, so do and observe whatever they tell you, but not the works they do. For they preach, but do not practice. They tie up heavy burdens, hard to bear, and lay them on people's shoulders, but they themselves are not willing to move them with their finger. (Matt. 23:2–4)

The Pharisees had convinced nearly everyone that they were the authorities on the Law of Moses, in both how to interpret and apply it. Jesus was saying that to the degree the Pharisees accurately interpreted Scripture, they should be obeyed. The problem was that they didn't obey it themselves. The law of God had always been about the heart, and we've started to see (and will see more clearly as we continue reading) that the Pharisees were not concerned about the state of their hearts before God; they were enamored by the authority they exercised. They were not really interested in living under God's authority themselves. They wanted to pick and choose the laws that suited them and avoid the ones that didn't. They wanted to add their own laws to God's law that they could use to lord over others. They were far more interested in monitoring the behavior of others than they were in sharing the burdens of others.

2. Religious hypocrites are more interested in impressing others than serving others.

> They do all their deeds to be seen by others. For they make their phylacteries broad and their fringes long, and they love the place of honor at feasts and the best seats in the synagogues and greetings in the marketplaces and being called rabbi by others. But you are not to be called rabbi, for you have one teacher, and you are all brothers. And call no man your father on earth, for you have one Father, who is in heaven. Neither be called instructors, for you have one instructor, the Christ. The greatest among you shall be your servant. Whoever exalts himself will be humbled, and whoever humbles himself will be exalted. (Matt. 23:5–12)

Notice the word "all" in verse 5. *All* the Pharisees' actions were polluted with pride. They dressed and accessorized themselves in ways that portrayed them as more devout than they really were. In Deuteronomy 6 and 11, Moses told God's people to bind God's words as a sign on their hand and on frontlets between their eyes. The Pharisees took this admonition *very* literally. Phylacteries were capsules in which tiny scrolls with Scripture passages from Exodus or Deuteronomy or other parts of the Law or Prophets were stuffed. They wore these phylacteries on their foreheads and on their arms. And apparently, they would make the phylacteries as wide as possible so that others would say, "Boy, he must be really committed; look how big that phylactery is." In Numbers 15, tassels had been commanded for the people of God to wear as reminders of God's commandments. The Pharisees, therefore, instructed their tailors to make their tassels extra long, so that when they walked through the streets, people would say, "Look how long that man's tassels are; he must be very holy."

When I was in high school, I was very involved in a youth ministry that was rather legalistic (which, I have to say, kept me out of a lot of trouble). I didn't listen to rock music or go to movies. And

I carried my Bible to school, mainly because I wanted to be able to say that I carried my Bible to school. I don't remember reading it all that much or sharing anything from it with anyone else. My Bible was an accessory that made me look more devoted to God than I really was. It turned out to be a sign of my hypocrisy.

The Pharisees loved it when they strode into the crowded synagogue in front of everyone else and took seats in the front that were reserved for them. It made them feel so very important. They loved the honorific titles that people gave to them—"Rabbi," "Father." They had no interest in being ordinary believers; no interest in being brothers and companions in the journey of faith. They wanted to be at the front of the pack, the recognized experts, the ones who had this life-with-God thing all figured out. What they were not at all interested in was being servants. They wanted to be impressive, not submissive. They wanted others to honor them, not to humble themselves before others. They were far more concerned about being perceived as holy than in being genuinely and pervasively holy.

In ancient writing, the most significant truth in a passage was often found in the center. That is the case with this passage in Matthew 23. Jesus hid the treasure at the center of his speech in verses 11–12: "The greatest among you shall be your servant. Whoever exalts himself will be humbled, and whoever humbles himself will be exalted." Before we continue with the rest of Jesus's indicators of religious hypocrisy, we must stop for a moment and consider the remedy for hypocrisy, the antithesis of hypocrisy, as found in these verses. The remedy for hypocrisy is servanthood and humility. Instead of adding to people's burdens, a servant seeks to share the load of other people's burdens. Instead of wrangling to get the seat of honor, a humble person willingly takes a back seat, sits on the floor, or works in the nursery. Instead of skillfully crafting a public image of spirituality or generosity, a humble person pursues a genuine relationship with the Holy Spirit in secret through private prayer. As they do, the Holy

Spirit fills them with contentment in the lower place, with lesser recognition, and with a willingness to delay the gratification of exaltation. Jesus was saying that a day would come when you will either be exalted because you chose to humble yourself in the here and now, or you will be humbled because you persisted in proud pretension.

If we want to do battle with our tendency toward arrogant hypocrisy, we're going to have to figure out how we can serve Christ by serving other people who have nothing to offer us, and then resist dropping reports of our service in conversation or in posts on social media. And, if we really want to walk in genuine repentance over the public portrayals of our "spirituality" in our past, James would say to us, "Confess your sins to one another and pray for one another, that you may be healed" (James 5:16). Hypocrisy loses its power when we're honest about the darkness in our own hearts in the presence of our brothers and sisters.

Recently I was preparing to speak at a big event, and I found myself twisted up inside about it. It wasn't so much the speaking that I was uptight about; it was my heart causing the problem. It was my sinful pride and my coveting the gifts and opportunities of some of the other speakers that was the problem. It's embarrassing to admit, but it's true. There is freedom in just putting it out there and naming it for what it is. Sin loses its power when we name it, and hypocrisy loses its foothold in our hearts when we become more interested in being holy than in being impressive. I've also found it helps to confess it to a good friend, inviting her to pray for me to forsake that sin, which is far better than complaining to a friend, hoping that she will join me in justifying that sin.

In Matthew 23, Jesus began his seven "woes"—seven indictments of the religious hypocrisy of the Pharisees—with, "But woe to you, scribes and Pharisees, hypocrites!" (Matt. 23:13). What does he mean by "woe"? Inherent in the word "woe" is heartbroken lament, an expression of grievous, horrified dread that essentially says, "How horrible it will be for you!" As Jesus considered the terrible judgment that was ahead for those who had embraced religious pretense instead of humble repentance, his passion was fueled by love. Inherent in his "woe" was an invitation to flee religious pretension to experience something real—a real relationship with God through his Son.

These days, people often label truth-telling and brokenhearted warnings of judgment as hate speech. But it is not unloving to warn people of certain disaster. If you can see that a bridge is out on a mountain pass that someone else is barreling toward, and you don't warn him, that is cruel. Likewise, because Jesus could see the bitter end the Pharisees were facing because of their ongoing rebellion and rejection of him, his words of warning were the epitome of love.

3. Religious hypocrites are more interested in imposing rules than in extending grace.

> But woe to you, scribes and Pharisees, hypocrites! For you shut the kingdom of heaven in people's faces. For you neither enter yourselves nor allow those who would enter to go in. (Matt. 23:13)

Have you ever had someone slam a door in your face? What vivid imagery Jesus uses when he speaks of shutting the door in the faces of those who longed for acceptance into the presence of God forever! These religious leaders should have been throwing open the door; instead they slammed the door labeled "holiness by grace" in people's faces even as they pushed them through the door labeled "holiness by trying harder." What a cruel thing to do.

4. Religious hypocrites are more interested in convincing others they're right than in being righteous.

> Woe to you, scribes and Pharisees, hypocrites! For you travel across sea and land to make a single proselyte, and when he

becomes a proselyte, you make him twice as much a child of hell as yourselves. (Matt. 23:15)

Catch the zeal with which the Pharisees spread their misguided religion. If we sign up to go on a mission trip in the twenty-first century, we can hop on a plane and get to a remote village in Africa in about 24 hours or less. But imagine the cost and the rigor of travel in the first century. These are the kinds of "mission trips" the Pharisees were taking. Think of the effort required to convince someone immersed in Greek mythology or pagan mysticism to follow the rabbinic law about ceremonial washing, to give up eating pork, and to count the number of steps they took on the Sabbath. How cruel to prey upon people willing to trust the word of those they thought were better versed in God's revelation than they were. Rather than impressing upon them the grace and mercy of God available to sinners, the Pharisees were imposing upon these converts to Pharisaic Judaism a lifelong burden of self-denial that would get them nowhere. These hypocrites got credit for making a convert, but ultimately and eternally it was a loss for everyone involved.

5. Religious hypocrites are more interested in righteousness that can be measured than in righteousness that matters.

> Woe to you, blind guides, who say, "If anyone swears by the temple, it is nothing, but if anyone swears by the gold of the temple, he is bound by his oath." You blind fools! For which is greater, the gold or the temple that has made the gold sacred? And you say, "If anyone swears by the altar, it is nothing, but if anyone swears by the gift that is on the altar, he is bound by his oath." You blind men! For which is greater, the gift or the altar that makes the gift sacred? So whoever swears by the altar swears by it and by everything on it. And whoever swears by the temple swears by it and by him who dwells in it. And whoever swears by heaven swears by the throne of God and by him who sits upon it.

> Woe to you, scribes and Pharisees, hypocrites! For you tithe mint and dill and cumin, and have neglected the weightier matters of the law: justice and mercy and faithfulness. These you ought to have done, without neglecting the others. You blind guides, straining out a gnat and swallowing a camel! (Matt. 23:16–24)

Five times in this passage Jesus described the Pharisees as blind. They were "blind guides" (v. 16) and "blind fools" (v. 17). What was it they couldn't see? They couldn't see the pathway to peace with God. It was not because the word from God that they diligently studied didn't reveal it. It was that they had stubbornly refused to see it. They had obstinately refused to see the truth. And they were not just blind; they were blind guides. They were intent on leading other people in their own crooked, never-going-to-be-good-enough and never-going-to-arrive path that led only to destruction.

In this passage we have a "three-image mosaic on majoring in minors."[10] And each image is meant to be a bit funny. First, consider "blind guides." Can you picture a blind guide? It sounds a little bit like a child's birthday party game. The idea of a blind guide is funny . . . at least it's funny until that blind guide leads you into a pit that consumes you.

The second image is of a word game. The Pharisees had come up with word tricks based on what they swore by that would get them out of following through on their commitments. You were only committed if you swore by the right thing. It reminds me of the childhood game "Simon Says," because it all comes down to the exact words used by the person giving instructions. It was this foolishness of the Pharisees that prompted Jesus to say, "Let what you say be simply 'Yes' or 'No'" (Matt. 5:37). Forget the games and be a person of your word.

The third image might be the funniest. To get it, we have to understand that both gnats and camels were considered unclean animals—animals that Jews did not eat. In order to keep from unintentionally ingesting an unclean dead animal, such as a microscopic bug that might have perished in an open vat of aging wine, the Pharisees strained their wine through a thin cloth. Jesus used this imagery of straining out a gnat but swallowing a camel to confront their efforts in rigorous tithing. They went through their spice racks, counting all the spices—*nine for me, one for God; nine for me, one for God*—while ignoring the weighty matters of God's law. What were the weighty matters of the law? Micah 6:8 asks the question, "What does the Lord require?" And the answer Micah gives is to love mercy, do justice, and walk humbly with God. The prophet Zechariah says that what really matters is that we render true judgments and show kindness and mercy to one another (Zech. 7:9). The Pharisees were ignoring these camel-sized commands. By tithing their spices and ignoring these weightier commands, it was like they were straining out a gnat but swallowing a camel. Their tithing of spices and straining for gnats was an exercise in missing the point. They had completely lost their sense of proportion in terms of what matters to God.

It gives a person pause, doesn't it? It makes me wonder: What have I turned into a big deal that really isn't that big of a deal to God? And what really matters to him that either doesn't matter to me enough or doesn't matter to me at all? What doesn't come up on my radar? Do I love what God loves and hate what he hates? Am I motivated by what matters to him or more motivated by my own interests, convenience, inclinations, and reputation?

Let's face it, we'd much rather be able to count and measure our way into favor with God than to feel the weight and work of what it means for us to extend mercy to people around us, to figure out how to practice justice when we'd rather enjoy an advantage, and to walk humbly with our God in a world of distraction and misdirection. It wasn't just hard for them. It's hard for us too.

6. Religious hypocrites are more interested in outward appearance than inward reality.

> Woe to you, scribes and Pharisees, hypocrites! For you clean the outside of the cup and the plate, but inside they are full of greed and self-indulgence. You blind Pharisee! First clean the inside of the cup and the plate, that the outside also may be clean.
>
> Woe to you, scribes and Pharisees, hypocrites! For you are like whitewashed tombs, which outwardly appear beautiful, but within are full of dead people's bones and all uncleanness. So you also outwardly appear righteous to others, but within you are full of hypocrisy and lawlessness. (Matt. 23:25–28)

Have you ever pulled out a rarely used teacup or goblet that had a dead bug in it? That's similar to the picture Jesus used here. A cup that is filthy on the inside illustrates a person who is filled with the contamination of sin on the inside. The Pharisees were very concerned about ritual purity, which they addressed through elaborate cleansing rituals so that they would appear to be clean to anyone observing. But they were unconcerned about the contamination of greed and the soiling of self-indulgence that had settled inside their lives.

After painting a picture of their inner contamination using the imagery of a dirty cup, Jesus drew upon a second familiar image to drive home his point. Jesus was speaking during the week when Jewish pilgrims were on their way to Jerusalem for Passover. The road would take them through areas where there were tombs of the prophets. If someone stumbling in the dark accidentally touched the tomb of a dead person, he would become ceremonially unclean and unable to participate in Passover. So the Jews put whitewash on the tombs to make them more easily seen in the dark. Jesus said that the Pharisees were like those whitewashed tombs. They looked good on the outside, but there was death inside. This got to the heart of the problem with the Pharisees. They were dead inside. Spiritually dead. Even though they tried to dress up and paint over their deadness.

Friends, this is the source of religious hypocrisy—spiritual deadness—a heart of stone that has not been fully transformed into a heart of flesh through the power of the Holy Spirit.

7. Religious hypocrites are more interested in silencing conviction than in responding to conviction.

> Woe to you, scribes and Pharisees, hypocrites! For you build the tombs of the prophets and decorate the monuments of the righteous, saying, "If we had lived in the days of our fathers, we would not have taken part with them in shedding the blood of the prophets." Thus you witness against yourselves that you are sons of those who murdered the prophets. (Matt. 23:29–31)

The Pharisees worked hard to rebuild, decorate, and maintain the tombs of the prophets. But Jesus was saying that if they wanted to honor the prophets, they should listen to what the prophets taught. The Pharisees thought they were in league with all that was good and right, but Jesus was saying that really they were in league with all their ancestors in the past who refused to take to heart the prophets' convicting words and instead sought to silence them. In fact, over the course of the next 48 hours, the Pharisees would do just what their ancestors had done to the prophets. They would seek to silence the ultimate prophet by carrying out their plot to put him to death.

So there we have it—a sevenfold indictment against religious hypocrites. And some of us have seen ourselves in some of these charges. We're feeling the "woe" of Jesus's warning. And we're wondering . . . is there any hope for hypocrites? Is there any hope for from-the-heart change? Is there any hope that someone who is blind to her own duplicity and lack of integrity could be healed of that blindness? "That would take a miracle," you say.

And you would be right. "That is not something I can do on my own," you say. That's exactly right. That's exactly what Jesus was trying to make clear to a Pharisee who visited him in the middle of the night.

Is There Any Hope for Hypocrites?

In John 3, we read about a Pharisee named Nicodemus, and his story offers hope to hypocritical people who want a real relationship with God.

> Now there was a man of the Pharisees named Nicodemus, a ruler of the Jews. This man came to Jesus by night and said to him, "Rabbi, we know that you are a teacher come from God, for no one can do these signs that you do unless God is with him." (John 3:1–2)

Nicodemus came to Jesus at night—perhaps so that no one would see him. But even if he had come in the middle of the day, Nicodemus came to Jesus in spiritual darkness as do all blind guides. But there's a glimmer of light. Nicodemus was not as dismissive of Jesus's miracles as his fellow Pharisees, who had assigned them to the power of Satan (John 8:48, 52). The miracles had seemingly convinced Nicodemus that Jesus was no ordinary teacher. He didn't really ask Jesus a question, but rather, put what he had figured out about Jesus out there for Jesus to respond to. In his response, Jesus told this blind guide what had to happen if he truly wanted to see:

> Jesus answered him, "Truly, truly, I say to you, unless one is born again he cannot see the kingdom of God." (John 3:3)

If Nicodemus was to have any hope of understanding who Jesus was, something had to happen—something supernatural. He had to be born a second time. Nicodemus, a respected religious leader, had come to investigate Jesus's miracles, and Jesus told him that if he did not experience a miracle, his religiosity would remain empty and useless. Unless something supernatural happened, Nicodemus would never experience freedom from hypocrisy and the joy of living with integrity.

Jesus didn't say, "One thing you might consider if you're wanting to improve yourself would be to be born again." He pointed out that Nicodemus's present condition was hopelessly unresponsive. There was no way Nicodemus could improve himself, study himself, or obey his way into God's good graces. He did not need "seven steps to becoming a person of integrity and sincerity." He did not need a little life coaching to get rid of his hypocritical tendencies. He needed a miracle.

Maybe as you're reading, you're beginning to recognize that what you need, more than going to church or becoming a better person or trying really hard to be more authentic, is a genuine miracle. What Nicodemus needed, and what you and I need, is not more religious activity or discipline. We need the miracle of newness in our essential being that only comes from God.

> Nicodemus said to him, "How can these things be?" Jesus answered him, "Are you the teacher of Israel and yet you do not understand these things? Truly, truly, I say to you, we speak of what we know, and bear witness to what we have seen, but you do not receive our testimony." (John 3:9–11)

What Jesus told Nicodemus about being born of the Spirit didn't fit with the Pharisees' categories for gaining favor with God through strict adherence to rabbinical tradition. At this point, Nicodemus was so blind he simply couldn't see his own need for repentance, let alone a need for miraculous whole-life cleansing and heart transformation. Nicodemus was like some of us. The wind of the Spirit often blows in our lives for a while before it completes its transforming, life-giving work.

Jesus brought his conversation with Nicodemus to a close by drawing upon an Old Testament image of salvation that pictured what Nicodemus needed to do to experience salvation.

No one has ascended into heaven except he who descended from heaven, the Son of Man. And as Moses lifted up the serpent in the wilderness, so must the Son of Man be lifted up, that whoever believes in him may have eternal life. (John 3:13–15)

This interaction between Jesus and Nicodemus ended without any evidence of belief on the part of Nicodemus, without any evidence of the miracle of regeneration and repentance taking place. But later, when the Son of Man was lifted up on a cross, we discover that the "whoever believes in him" included this Pharisee, Nicodemus. We read again about Nicodemus in the context of the story of Joseph of Arimathea asking for the body of Jesus after the crucifixion.

And when evening had come, since it was the day of Preparation, that is, the day before the Sabbath, Joseph of Arimathea, a respected member of the council, who was also himself looking for the kingdom of God, took courage and went to Pilate and asked for the body of Jesus. (Mark 15:42–44)

John tells us that this Joseph was "a disciple of Jesus but secretly for fear of the Jews" (John 19:38). It sounds as if Joseph was not only friends with the Pharisees, he feared the Pharisees, and his heart had been shaped by the example of the Pharisees. He was a bit of a religious hypocrite too. Up to this point, Joseph had not been interested in being identified with Jesus. It was simply too dangerous. Then we read that Joseph "took courage" and went to Pilate.

Unless relatives claimed the body of an executed criminal within an hour of execution, the body was taken to one of the two cemeteries outside Jerusalem and dumped into a common pit. Clearly, no family was coming forward. None of the twelve disciples showed up to ask for the body of Jesus. But there was Joseph.

And evidently Joseph was not alone in his mission to honor Jesus with a burial fit for a king instead of a criminal. John tells us, "Nicodemus also, who earlier had come to Jesus by night, came bringing a mixture of myrrh and aloes, about seventy-five pounds in weight. So they took the body of Jesus and bound it in linen cloths with the spices, as is the burial custom of the Jews" (John 19:38–40). Nicodemus no longer wanted to lay heavy burdens of strict law keeping on people's shoulders. Instead, he was bearing the burden of seventy-five pounds of spices on his own shoulders. Seventy-five pounds. When you fly on a plane, your bag can't be over 50 pounds. Have you ever heaved a suitcase on the scale and crossed your fingers that it wouldn't be over 50 pounds? Picture the wealthy, influential Joseph and the avoid-touching-a-dead-body-at-all-costs Pharisee, Nicodemus. Try to picture in your mind this wealthy man and this religious leader going to the other side of the tracks, outside the gates of the city, to where common criminals were crucified. Perhaps one of them climbed up a ladder by the cross and pulled out the nails one by one that held Jesus to the cross, wiping away the blood and the spit, and embraced the lifeless body of the crucified King. Then they packed the dead body of Jesus with 75 pounds of spices, wrapped him in the finest linen money could buy, and put Jesus's body in Joseph's never-used tomb.

Jesus had wanted to gather hypocrites like Joseph and Nicodemus to himself as a hen gathers her brood under her wings. His list of woes to the Pharisees ended with a brokenhearted lament: "O Jerusalem, Jerusalem, the city that kills the prophets and stones those who are sent to it! How often would I have gathered your children together as a hen gathers her brood under her wings, and you were not willing!" (Matt. 23:37). But now these two were willing! In reaching out to take hold of Christ, they discovered that they had been taken hold of by Christ.

To take hold of Christ is to take hold of the only person whose motives are always perfectly pure, the only person who kept the law perfectly, and the only person who humbled himself completely. Rather than tie up heavy burdens and put them on people's shoulders, Jesus said, "Come to me, all who labor and are heavy laden, and I will give you rest" (Matt. 11:28–29). Rather than insisting on being honored by others, Jesus humbled himself to wash the feet of others. Rather than shutting the door to the kingdom of heaven in people's faces, Jesus offered himself as the door, the way into the kingdom of heaven.

There is hope for hypocrites who will place themselves at the foot of the cross, where Christ took upon himself our sin of hypocrisy and the shame we feel over it. As we take hold of Christ, his purity begins to flow into our lives, his blood washes away our impurity, and his perspective about what really matters begins to shape our perspective about what really matters.

Some of us have spent a lifetime trying to cover up the ugliness of the interior of our lives, and we've gotten good at it. But there is hope for hypocrites. It is found in the gospel—the gospel of Christ's perfectly righteous life, his atoning death, his glorious resurrection, and his all-sufficient, forgiving, delivering grace that flows into our lives as we become joined to him by faith that changes us from the inside out. The grace of Jesus, the only perfectly sincere person who has ever lived, is able to transform the worst hypocrite into a humble saint.

> Come, ye sinners, poor and needy,
> Weak and wounded, sick and sore!
> Jesus ready stands to save you,
> Full of pity, love and power.
>
> I will arise and go to Jesus,
> He will embrace me in His arms;
> In the arms of my dear Savior,
> O, there are ten thousand charms.
>
> Let not conscience let you linger,
> Nor of fitness fondly dream;
> All the fitness he requireth
> Is to feel your need of him.

Come, ye weary, heavy-laden,
Lost and ruined by the fall;
If you tarry till you're better,
You will never come at all.[11]

5

THE CROOK

I think I was only four or five years old when, during one of those long Sunday night invitations at our Baptist church, I told my parents I wanted to go forward. My parents wisely made an appointment for me to speak to our pastor instead. I can remember sitting in his office and being asked if I knew what it meant to be lost. I thought about being lost in a forest or a shopping mall. But I don't think that was the answer he was looking for. Maybe I didn't yet understand what it really meant to be lost.

I often wonder, when I hear people singing the song "Amazing Grace"[12] in all kinds of settings, if they really think that they are now or ever have been a "wretch"? When they sing, "I once was lost, but now I'm found; was blind, but now I see," I want to ask, "In what way were you lost, and how or by whom were you found?"

Until we have a sense of what it means to be lost, I'm not sure we can come to any real sense of who Jesus is and why he came into this world or why we need him. Our lostness is at the very center of these things.

In his Gospel, Luke uses two statements of Jesus that correspond to make the mission of Jesus clear. One is near the beginning of Jesus's three years of ministry, as he called his first disciple, a tax collector named Levi. Seeing who was invited to the party afterward, the Pharisees were incredulous that Jesus would sit down to share a meal with such people—people whose sins made them untouchable and ineligible for grace in the Pharisees' minds. In response, Jesus made clear why he had come: "I have not come to call the righteous but sinners to repentance" (Luke 5:32).

Then, near the end of Jesus's ministry, on his last ministry stop before his final week in Jerusalem, which culminated in his crucifixion, Jesus once again offered his personal mission statement: "The Son of Man came to seek and to save the lost" (Luke 19:10).

Jesus came to call sinners to repentance, to seek and save the lost.

So what does it mean to be lost? I think it is to have no anchor, no direction, no purpose, no destination in sight. It is to wander through life aimless, disconnected, and confused, always hoping that the next purchase, the next experience, the next vacation, the next milestone, the next high, the next promotion, or the next romance will fill the void. Most profoundly, to be lost is to be adrift, untethered, and cut off from the only sure and steadfast anchor for the soul (Heb. 6:18–19). It is to be outside of and alienated from the only person who can provide rest for your soul. It is to be vulnerable to being forever lost.

Jesus's climactic purpose statement—that he had come to seek and to save the lost—comes at the end of a four-chapter chunk of text that is all about lostness. The section begins with three parables about lost things—a lost coin, a lost sheep, and a lost son (or really, two lost sons). From there, Luke introduces us to a series of people who are lost: Pharisees who are lost in their love of money and human achievement (16:14); a rich man who finds himself lost in the torment of Hades (16:23); lepers lost in social alienation and sickness (17:11–13); people lost in the ordinary concerns of eating and drinking, buying and selling, planting and building, unaware of the coming judgment (17:27);

Pharisees lost in empty religiosity (18:9–12); a tax collector lost in his sense of shame (18:13); a rich young ruler lost in his love of money (18:18–23); and a blind man lost in darkness and poverty (18:35). The series culminates in the story of the person we are going to focus on now. Zacchaeus, the chief tax collector, lived in Jericho but was lost in greed and corruption, lost in loneliness and meaninglessness.

The Setting

The story of this lost man begins with Jesus coming to town or, more accurately, passing through town.

He entered Jericho and was passing through. (Luke 19:1)

Jericho, called the "City of Palms,"[13] was considered a little paradise full of the pleasant fragrances of cypress flowers, rose gardens, and balsam plantations. It was also strategically located on the caravan route from Damascus to Arabia, making it a city of active commerce. The skyline of the city was dominated by four fortresses, which made it a center of military activity. Just think of all the goods and services, real estate and military business, let alone all the consumer goods that went in and out of Jericho. Imagine how much money a person could make if given a percentage of all that business!

This was the time of year when processions of people made their way from the surrounding areas to be in Jerusalem for Passover, and many of these groups or processions passed through Jericho on the way to the feast. On this particular day, it seemed that word spread about a group of people passing through Jericho on the way to Jerusalem that included Jesus of Nazareth, the one who had performed healing miracles throughout Galilee and taught with authority. Then people heard that he'd done one of his healing miracles on his way into town—he had given sight to the blind man who always sat by the roadside begging. People came out of their homes to get a glimpse of Jesus. They lined the streets to watch for him. Maybe he would tell one of his stories. Maybe he would go to someone's house. Maybe someone else would get healed.

The Scoundrel

Someone unexpected, and honestly unwanted, was about to join the crowd watching for Jesus.

> And behold, there was a man named Zacchaeus. He was a chief tax collector and was rich. (Luke 19:2)

Evidently when his parents gave him the name Zacchaeus, which means "just" or "pure," they imagined him growing up and being a man of integrity and purity. Instead, he grew up to be a man whose life revolved around constant corruption. How do we know that? He was a tax collector, and he was rich. Tax collecting in Israel was synonymous with corruption.

One had to be rich in order to become a collector of taxes for Rome. Wealthy Jewish citizens purchased the rights from Rome to collect land, poll, and customs taxes in certain cities or regions. They put in a bid for the taxes they estimated they could collect, and if they won the bid, then they got to set the tax rates and rules in that region. They were free to collect as much as they wanted above what they promised to send to Rome, and taxpayers had no recourse or relief.

Jewish people already resented Rome and the heavy tax burden Rome placed on them. So they really hated the Jewish people who collaborated with Rome to take advantage of them. Tax collectors, therefore, weren't allowed in the temple or synagogues. They weren't even allowed to testify in court, as they were considered thoroughly crooked and corrupt.

And Zacchaeus wasn't just a tax collector; he was a *chief* tax collector. He would have had a host of lower-level tax collectors working for him, and he got a piece of it all. We could call him "the kingpin of the Jericho tax cartel."[14]

Zacchaeus might have been rich, but all the money in the world couldn't buy what Zacchaeus needed most deep in his soul. He was lost in greed, materialism, and the misuse of power. Who knows how long it had been since he'd been to the synagogue and heard the words of the Law and Prophets read, the words that bring life and give direction and meaning?

The Seeker

Maybe it was emptiness or loneliness that prompted Zacchaeus to risk mixing with crowds of people who hated him. Or maybe it was simple curiosity. Luke writes that "he was seeking to see who Jesus was" (Luke 19:3).

Perhaps Zacchaeus had heard about what happened out in the wilderness where John the Baptist preached to crowds of people and offered a baptism of repentance. Luke records, "Tax collectors also came to be baptized." They were unwelcome at the synagogue but welcome in the waters of baptism. The newly baptized tax collectors asked John, "Teacher, what shall we do?" And he said to them, "Collect no more than you are authorized to do" (Luke 3:12–13). John was explaining how they should demonstrate their repentance—not by leaving the business of tax collecting but by conducting that business fairly and honestly.

I wonder if some of those tax collectors who were baptized by John worked for Zacchaeus or in neighboring towns. Did they come home and begin to do business differently? And though their bank accounts might have been smaller, did Zacchaeus notice that they were actually happier? Did he wonder if Jesus could offer him that same kind of happiness?

Maybe Zacchaeus knew or had heard about the tax collector named Levi who was sitting at his tax booth one day when Jesus simply said to him, "Follow me," and Levi left everything to follow Jesus. Perhaps Zacchaeus was curious about what Levi saw in Jesus—something so appealing, someone so compelling that it would be worth leaving a lucrative trade just to be with him.

Perhaps Zacchaeus had heard some of the stories Jesus had told as he traveled from Galilee to Jericho—particularly the one about the Pharisee and the tax collector. Pharisees were always the heroes of the stories in Zacchaeus's day, and tax collectors were always the butt of jokes. But not in the story Jesus had told. In his story, the self-righteous Pharisee was shown to be an outsider with God while the self-aware tax collector was welcomed in. I wonder if Zacchaeus heard that story and if it might have planted a flicker of hope that he could actually find peace with God instead of waking up every day and going to bed every night with a troubled conscience and no access to cleansing for it.

Perhaps he had heard that the Pharisees liked to call Jesus "friend of tax collectors and sinners" (Matt. 11:19; Luke 7:34). And maybe he wondered if Jesus would be his friend too.

The next couple of verses capture most of what we remember when we think of Zacchaeus—that he was a wee little man who climbed up in a sycamore tree, for the Lord he wanted to see.

> And he was seeking to see who Jesus was, but on account of the crowd he could not, because he was small in stature. So he ran on ahead and climbed up into a sycamore tree to see him, for he was about to pass that way. (Luke 19:3–4)

Picture some rich, powerful crime boss you've seen in the news. He doesn't run anywhere; he struts. Can you imagine one of those guys shedding his dignity to climb a tree? Not just that, but climbing a tree to see a poor carpenter from Nazareth? It sounds like something a child would do, not a rich and powerful man. In the previous chapter, we read that Jesus said, "Truly, I say to you, whoever does not receive the kingdom of God like a child shall not enter it" (Luke 18:17). Zacchaeus seemed to be positioning himself to enter the kingdom of God.

Why did he have to climb a tree? We know he was short, and there was a crowd, but usually a short person can work his way to the front of the crowd. It's likely that no one in this crowd would have had any interest in making way for Zacchaeus. He was a crook and a traitor. He had had his way with their goods, always taking some for himself. His fine clothes did not impress them because they knew those clothes were purchased with what he took from them. They hated him. So he bypassed them, avoiding their tangible disgust, and positioned himself to see Jesus.

> And when Jesus came to the place, he looked up and said to him, "Zacchaeus, hurry and come down, for I must stay at your house today." (Luke 19:5)

Jesus was walking along, and the crowds were pressing in around him at eye level, calling out to him. But then Jesus stopped and looked up. He looked past the crowd, past the indignity of a man in a tree, past Zacchaeus's sinful reputation and into his eyes, even into his heart.

Zacchaeus had come seeking to see who Jesus was. What he didn't know was that Jesus had come to Jericho seeking him. The primary seeker in this story was actually not Zacchaeus; it was Jesus. Jesus was the good shepherd, and when he turned his gaze away from the crowd gathered around him, he was leaving the ninety-nine to go after this lost sheep named Zacchaeus.

Zacchaeus had been seen, and he was being sought after. And isn't that what we all long for?

Zacchaeus heard Jesus calling him by name. "He knows my name!" In that moment, something began to happen in Zacchaeus's heart. He had never heard of the doctrine of effectual calling. He just knew that Jesus had called to him and told him to hurry down, and now there was nothing he wanted more than to hurry down and have Jesus come into his house and into his life.

To have a meal and stay overnight in someone's home in that day meant more than just a meal. It indicated acceptance and connection. Jesus wanted to be savingly connected to Zacchaeus.

The Salvation

> So he hurried and came down and received him joyfully. (Luke 19:6)

Once again, there was something childlike about Zacchaeus's response to Jesus. This powerful, rich man was sliding down the tree and rushing to make things ready for his guest.

And he was not just in a hurry. He was happy. Jesus had seen him and called him. Jesus was entering into his home and into his life, and Zacchaeus was happy. He was beginning to understand what must have motivated Levi to leave the tax-gathering business to be with Jesus.

Zacchaeus was not naïve about what receiving Jesus would mean for him—what it would cost him. And he was still happy. In this way, his response was the opposite of the rich young ruler from the previous chapter in Luke's Gospel. Jesus's interaction with the rich young ruler ended with the rich man going away sad (Luke 18:24). Not Zacchaeus. He was taking Jesus home, and he was happy about what that was going to mean for his heart and his life. He was being set free from the greed that he had thought would finance his happiness but that had failed to deliver.

While Zacchaeus was happy that Jesus was coming home with him, no one else in town was happy about it.

> And when they saw it, they all grumbled, "He has gone in to be the guest of a man who is a sinner." (Luke 19:7)

Of all the people Jesus might have stayed with in town, and Jesus made a beeline for Zacchaeus's house? Didn't Jesus know how crooked and corrupt Zacchaeus was, what a scoundrel he was? What's interesting about this story is that a few minutes before, when Jesus healed the blind beggar on the way into town, "all the people, when they saw it, gave praise to God" (Luke 18:43). They were fine if Jesus stuck to seeking and saving the kind of lost people they approved of. But they did not approve of his meddling with those at Zacchaeus's level of lostness. It was fine if Jesus saved someone they had a soft spot for, but not when he saved someone they despised; someone who had hurt and stolen from them.

Luke didn't see fit to record Jesus's conversation over dinner with Zacchaeus. We just get to hear the seemingly public announcements they both made, perhaps during or after the dinner.

> And Zacchaeus stood and said to the Lord, "Behold, Lord, the half of my goods I give to the poor. And if I have defrauded anyone of anything, I restore it fourfold." (Luke 19:8)

This is the first time Zacchaeus spoke in this short story, and his first two words were telling. "Behold, Lord." In a sense he was saying, "Take a good look at me, Lord. I want you to see how having you in my life is no small thing to me. It's changing me. It's changing everything about my life. The idol of money no longer has its hold on my soul, and therefore I'm finding that I can loosen my grip on my wallet. The love you are showing to me makes me want to show that same kind of love to my neighbors."

Earlier he wanted to see who Jesus was, and now it was clear that he had seen who Jesus was. Jesus is Lord, and Zacchaeus wanted him to be Lord of his house, Lord of his money, Lord of his business practices, and Lord over everything. Jesus was not just an interesting religious figure to him. He was not merely a "friend of tax collectors and sinners"—he was Lord of this tax collector, friend of this sinner, and Savior of this sinner.

So first off, Zacchaeus said he was going to give away half of his net worth to the poor. There's no evidence Jesus told him to do this. Zacchaeus's heart was changed, and he wanted to do this. His motive was love, absent of the old greed. He was probably going to have to sell that big house they were having dinner in. He was probably not going to be able to afford to keep living the same lifestyle he had been living. But he was all in. And there was more! He was going to go back through the books and make a list of every person he had defrauded over the years. And he was not just going to give back what he shouldn't have taken. He was going to give them *four times* the amount he shouldn't have taken.

Where did Zacchaeus come up with this idea of restoring four-fold whatever he had defrauded? To obey God's command according to the Law of Moses regarding restitution would mean that he should return twice what he took (Exodus 22). But Zacchaeus wasn't simply trying to obey the letter of the law. Grace was at work in his heart, and he wanted to do more. He would give them all four times what he had taken from them.

He was not trying to buy his way into heaven. He was not trying to score religious points. He was making choices about his life out of a desire to conform to the ways of Jesus. His restitution wasn't the result of the law coming down on him but grace at work in him. Sinclair Ferguson has said, "When your heart is given over to the Lord Jesus, it's amazing what falls out of your hands because it has fallen out of your heart."[15]

Zacchaeus was not just saying, "Sorry if I hurt you." He was saying, "I know that I hurt you, and I'm taking responsibility to make it right." He was living out genuine repentance. Genuine repentance often calls for radical change.

- ✦ Maybe it means you move out from living with your boyfriend or stop sleeping with him.
- ✦ Maybe you get rid of the television because you no longer want your life to revolve around it, and you know that will require radical action.
- ✦ Maybe it means you return some things you've pilfered from the office or count up and pay back the amount you've dishonestly added to your expense reports over the years.
- ✦ Maybe it means that you apologize to the people who work for you or with you for the way you've treated them.
- ✦ Maybe you apologize to your parents or your siblings about the way you've talked about them or to them, or for not talking to them at all.

✝ Maybe you walk into the police station and ask them to take down your confession.

It's not that you decide to become a more moral person; it's that you've become a new person, a new creation; you have new habits, new tastes, new desires, new opinions, new joys, and new passions. Grace allows you to be transparent. You can admit your sin because you know you're savingly connected to the one who forgives sin. Grace makes you want to conform your life to Jesus— to treat people like he treats them, to value what he values, to hate what he hates.

> And Jesus said to him, "Today salvation has come to this house, since he also is a son of Abraham." (Luke 19:9)

When we read that salvation has come to this house, we have to remember that only a short time before this, Jesus had said it was easier for a camel to go through the eye of a needle than for a rich man to enter the kingdom of God. In other words, it was impossible. When he said that, his disciples asked, "Then who can be saved?" And Jesus said, "What is impossible with man is possible with God" (Luke 18:25–27). So when Jesus says that salvation has come to Zacchaeus, a rich man, we realize that the impossible has happened. It's a miracle. It's a different kind of miracle than leprosy being healed or blind eyes being made to see. It's an internal miracle of the soul.

Zacchaeus probably didn't have the words to explain what happened to him. He just knew that nothing was the same. He didn't know all the aspects of the salvation that had come to him. He probably didn't know the word *regeneration*. He just knew that the deadness toward God was gone, and there was an energizing newness to his life. He probably didn't know the word *conversion*, but faith and repentance seemed the most obvious and natural responses to what he had seen in Jesus. In fact, this was why Jesus called him a "son of Abraham." Paul would later write that "it is those of faith who are the sons of Abraham" (Gal. 3:7). "Abraham believed the Lord, and he counted it to him as righteousness" (Gen. 15:6), and in this way Zacchaeus was looking a lot like his father, Abraham. Zacchaeus might not have known the word *justification*, but the righteousness of Christ had been applied to his account, and there was now no condemnation for him in God's eyes. He probably didn't know the word *sanctification*. Zacchaeus just knew that he wanted to be holy as God is holy. He knew he simply couldn't keep holding on to his sin and take hold of Jesus as Savior at the same time. This was day one of a new life, and he was not wasting any time putting sin to death in his life.

Zacchaeus was not saying he was going to resign as chief tax collector. He was likely going to keep collecting taxes, but he was going to do it honestly and fairly. And the other tax collectors were probably not going to like it. He was going to make them look worse, if that was even possible. He was going to demand that everyone who worked for him begin collecting taxes with integrity. The change that began in Zacchaeus's heart was going to have an impact on his whole business and the entire community.

Zacchaeus probably didn't know the word *perseverance*, but he was going to persevere in living out this newness of life. How do we know? We know because Luke surely wouldn't have included this story as the capstone to the ministry of Jesus in his Gospel if Zacchaeus had gone back on his promises, if he had gone back to his old way of life and to his old ways of greed. But the more obvious way we know Zacchaeus would persevere is because Jesus announced that salvation had come to him. If salvation had come to Zacchaeus, it would not leave him, it would not leak out of him. It would keep him. He would surely spend the rest of his life working out his salvation with fear and trembling (Phil. 2:12). And, my friend, if God has accomplished this miracle of salvation in your life, you can be sure that it will not be undone. The Spirit has sealed you to Christ. Nothing and no one can separate you.

Of course, Zacchaeus probably couldn't have used any of those words to describe all the aspects of the salvation that came to him that day. Perhaps all he could say to explain the change was that he had gone up the tree seeking Jesus, discovered that apparently Jesus had come seeking him, and that he would never be the same. From then on, Zacchaeus would have been able to pinpoint the day when he went from lost to found, from damned to saved, from crook to cleansed, from spiritually dead to spiritually alive.

Has there been a day when salvation came to you? You may or may not know when it happened, but if you are spiritually alive rather than dead, there was a moment when that happened. How do you know if it happened? If you are spiritually alive, there will be evidence in your life of salvation's newness, salvation's repentance, salvation's sanctification and perseverance. If you've been made alive spiritually, you'll be joyful about having Jesus in your life. You'll want to fellowship with him around his table. You'll be willing to come clean about the corruption in your own life—the corruption that has worked its way into your financial dealings, your sexual desires, perhaps even your ministry motives. You'll leap at the chance to set things right with those you've wronged rather than simply insist on "moving on." You'll be open to radical change to bring your life into conformity to Christ.

The Savior

By the time Zacchaeus finished paying people back, perhaps he was left with nothing. Yet he had everything—everything that mattered. "For you know the grace of our Lord Jesus Christ, that though he was rich, yet for your sake he became poor, so that you by his poverty might become rich" (2 Cor. 8:9). Having Jesus as his Lord and Savior meant there was a richness to Zacchaeus's life that far surpassed the money he once had in his accounts. He had an inheritance, "an inheritance that is imperishable, undefiled, and unfading, kept in heaven for [him]" (1 Pet. 1:4).

Even though Zacchaeus gave away much of his wealth as a response to the salvation that came to him, that salvation didn't actually cost Zacchaeus anything. But it cost Jesus everything. "For you were bought with a price" (1 Cor. 6:20.) "You were ransomed from the futile ways inherited from your forefathers, not with perishable things such as silver or gold, but with the precious blood of Christ, like that of a lamb without blemish or spot" (1 Pet. 1:18–19).

Jesus journeyed on from Jericho to Jerusalem, where "like a sheep he was led to the slaughter" (Acts 8:32). In Jericho, Jesus had identified with sinners by eating with a man who climbed up a tree. But in Jerusalem, he identified with sinners by allowing himself to be eaten up by sin as he hung on a tree. On the cross, Jesus took upon himself all the corruption of Zacchaeus. He took upon himself the corruption of all of us who are willing to receive him joyfully into the center of our lives.

If you're hiding from Jesus, you must know that Jesus is standing at the foot of whatever tree you're hiding in. He's saying, "Come down. Today is the day. I'm here. I came for you. You can leave the ranks of the lost and join the fellowship of the found, the forgiven."

I've found a Friend, O, such a Friend!
He loved me ere I knew Him;
He drew me with the cords of love,
And thus He bound me to Him.
And round my heart still closely twine
Those ties which naught can sever,
For I am His, and He is mine,
Forever and forever.

I've found a Friend, O, such a Friend!
He bled, He died to save me;
And not alone the gift of life,
But His own self He gave me.
Naught that I have my own I call,

I hold it for the Giver;
My heart, my strength, my life, my all,
Are His, and His forever.

I've found a Friend, O, such a Friend!
So kind, and true, and tender,
So wise a Counselor and Guide,
So mighty a Defender!
From Him who loves me now so well,
What power my soul can sever?
Shall life or death, or earth or hell?
No! I am His forever.[16]

6

THE OPPORTUNIST

There are few things more frustrating than to feel that our time has been wasted. We hate it when our money is wasted. We hate it when we buy the fancy ingredients for a special dish and then leave it on the stove too long so that it is burned to a crisp and goes straight into the trash. Or when we buy a new shirt and it ends up with ink or mascara or ketchup on it the first time we wear it, and the stain just won't come out. Or when we keep closing the door behind our kids in the summer because they leave it open, wasting all that expensive, conditioned air.

Years ago when David and I were newly married, we went to visit some friends who were in medical school. I took along my portable sewing machine, and we spent the day on Saturday making curtains for their apartment. And then someone (who shall remain nameless) got confused and ended up cutting through the middle of the almost-completed curtains. We had to go buy more material and start over. Wasted effort. Wasted time. Wasted resources.

But as frustrating as wasted time or effort can be, a far greater tragedy is a wasted life.

In this chapter, we're going to look closely at two people. One of them wasted away years of opportunity. He lived what proved to be a wasted life and died a tragic death. The other person was accused of being wasteful. Yet what appeared to many around her to be wasteful extravagance was actually wise acknowledgment of what (or who) is supremely valuable. As we compare these two people, we'll discover that there is a way to spend the capital of our lives that may appear wasteful to the world around us, but proves to be a beautiful way to live, a meaningful investment, an appropriate response to the most generous gift ever given.

Wasted Years

The lists of the twelve apostles, which we find in three of the Gospels, each begin with the name of Simon Peter and finish with the name of Judas Iscariot. "Judas" was a common name in that day, drawn from the Hebrew name Judah. Perhaps "Iscariot" had to do with the town in Judah where Judas was born and brought up. Other than the fact that his father was Simon Iscariot, the biblical record doesn't reveal much about this always-last-in-the-list disciple.

But we do know a lot about what his three years with Jesus were like. From what we know of the experiences of all the disciples as a group, we know that Judas was in the boat when Jesus calmed the storm. He helped serve when Jesus fed thousands of people with a few loaves and fish. Judas was given the authority and power to cast out demons and call people to repentance when Jesus sent the disciples out in twos to various cities. That's interesting to think about, isn't it? Because we know where the story of Judas is headed, we begin to realize that evidently it is possible for a person to have extraordinary gifts, even power in ministry, and yet lack saving grace. Evidently it is possible for God to work through the lives of people who have not experienced the profound work of conversion, regeneration, justification and ongoing sanctification in their own lives.

Judas heard Jesus tell the parable about the treasure hidden in a field that a man, with joy, went and sold all that he had to buy it. Judas heard the parable of the merchant in search of fine pearls who, finding one pearl of great value, went and sold all that he had to buy it. Did Judas understand what Jesus meant? Did he understand that Jesus himself is the treasure, the pearl worth off-loading everything you have of worldly value so you can have him?

He heard Jesus tell the parables of the sheep and the goats, and the good seed and the weeds, explaining that "the good seed is the sons of the kingdom. The weeds are the sons of the evil one, and the enemy who sowed them is the devil" (Matt. 13:38–39). Did Judas ever ask himself, "Am I a sheep or a goat?" or "Am I good seed or a weed?"

He heard Peter confess that Jesus was indeed the Christ. And he heard Jesus follow up on that confession, saying, "If anyone would come after me, let him deny himself and take up his cross and follow me. For whoever would save his life will lose it, but whoever loses his life for my sake will find it" (Matt. 16:24–25). Was that when Judas began to wonder if his close association with Jesus was really going to work in his favor, or if his years of following would prove to be an enormous waste of time and sacrifice?

Twelve men in human history were given the opportunity to spend three intimate years with Jesus. And just think of the fruit that was born in the lives of eleven of those men—the fruit of the gospel going out from Jerusalem, to Judea, to Samaria and to the ends of the earth; the fruit of the Gospels and epistles written; the fruit of their leadership in establishing and guiding the early church. So much fruit! But then there was Judas. In his life, this privilege bore no fruit. What a waste—wasted years, wasted privilege.

Jesus had said in the Sermon on the Mount, "No one can serve two masters, for either he will hate the one and love the other, or he will be devoted to the one and despise the other. You cannot serve God and money" (Matt 6:24). I wonder if he looked at Judas when he said it. Somewhere along the way, Judas became more devoted to money than to Jesus. And yet, all that devotion proved to be wasted devotion because Judas ended up losing everything. *Everything.*

But maybe we should give him a bit of a break. It had to have been frustrating to be the treasurer of a group in which opportunities to bring in game-changing gifts were squandered. Imagine his frustration when he overhead Jesus telling that rich man to sell everything he owned and give it to . . . the poor. "Why didn't he tell that guy to give it to us?" he must have said under his breath. Perhaps Judas even convinced himself that he would have made wise use of all that money. But we know better. We know that Judas was a thief. He was lining his pockets with the little bit of money that came into the shared purse of this band of disciples of Jesus. Paul wrote the love of money is a root of all kinds of evil. And surely Judas's love for money proved to be the root of the evil that eventually invaded him and ultimately destroyed him.

The first time we hear Judas speak, and really, the first time we observe him in action, is at a dinner party just six days before Jesus was crucified. If Judas had ever been sincere in his devotion to Jesus, it was clearly a thing of the past on this night.

Wasted Resources?

"Six days before the Passover, Jesus therefore came to Bethany, where Lazarus was, whom Jesus had raised from the dead. So they gave a dinner for him there. Martha served, and Lazarus was one of those reclining with him at table" (John 12:1–2). We're told in Matthew's account of this story that this dinner took place at Simon the leper's house. Imagine being around the table with Simon, who had only recently been quarantined because of his leprosy, but was now healed. Lazarus had been in the grave just a short time before, but now he was resurrected and reclining at the table, engaged in animated conversation with his friends.

Jesus was sharing a meal with two living, breathing recipients of his healing, resurrecting power. As Mary sat and listened in on the laughter and love around the table, she must have been waiting for the right moment to demonstrate her profound gratitude to Jesus for what he had done for her family. He had wept with them in their grief and then called to their brother in the grave. Lazarus had walked out of the grave alive again. He came home again.

Jesus had said, "I am the resurrection and the life. Whoever believes in me, though he die, yet shall he live, and everyone who lives and believes in me shall never die. Do you believe this?" (John 11:25–26). Mary did believe. She wanted to lavish her gratitude in a tangible way on the one who had not only brought her brother back to life but had promised that all who believed in him would never die.

> Mary therefore took a pound of expensive ointment made from pure nard, and anointed the feet of Jesus and wiped his feet with her hair. The house was filled with the fragrance of the perfume. (John 12:3)

Mary had been keeping a very special flask of ointment made from the root and spike of the nard plant, which was grown in India. The purity of this ointment, combined with the distance it had traveled and its limited quantity, made it incredibly valuable. Perhaps it was a family heirloom that they had never expected would actually be opened but would stay sealed, passed down in the family.

I looked on the Neiman Marcus website to find their most expensive bottle of perfume. It looks like it would be Jen Patou Joy, which is $1,800 for one ounce. It takes 28 dozen roses and 10,600 jasmine flowers to make a single bottle. Only fifty limited edition bottles are made each year. So, if you bought a pound of it (sixteen one-ounce bottles), it would cost you almost $30,000.

We don't have to guess how much the flask of ointment Mary brought out was worth because Judas said as much in verse 5. "Why was this ointment not sold for three hundred denarii?" he asked. This was an amount just short of a year's wages. What would a year's worth of income be in your family? Can you imagine having a flask of perfume that cost that much? It would have to be a very special occasion, a very valuable person, to get you to open that flask and use that perfume.

Judas was probably fine when Mary started pouring a little bit of it on Jesus's head. But then she kept pouring and kept pouring. It was running down his head, through his beard, over his whole body, and pooling around his feet. When the last drop was poured, she began wiping his feet with her hair.

This was too much for Judas to take! "But Judas Iscariot, one of his disciples (he who was about to betray him), said, 'Why was this ointment not sold for three hundred denarii and given to the poor?'" (John 12:4–5). To Mary, it was the value of the perfume that made what she did profoundly worthwhile. But to Judas, the value of the perfume was what made her actions seem a complete and total waste.

When Judas said it should have been sold and the money given to the poor, it sounded like a moral response, but really it was Judas's personal greed masquerading as altruism. He posed as a friend of the poor, when really he cared little for anyone but himself. He had failed to grasp who Jesus was and had no gratitude for what Jesus had done or had said he was about to do; so to Judas, this outpouring of love made no sense. His heart was stone-cold toward Jesus. He had heard talk of the priests' plot to put Jesus to death and had begun to wonder if perhaps all this was all going to end very badly and if the past three years of his life had been huge a waste of time. Jesus was going to die, and he was going to be left looking like a fool with nothing in his bank account to show for his investment of three years of his life.

If we thought for a minute that Judas cared about the poor, our narrator, John, reveals the real source of Judas's frustration with Mary's extravagance. "He said this, not because he cared about the poor, but because he was a thief, and having charge of the money bag he used to help himself to what was put into it" (John 12:6).

Now we can see how his heart had become so hard. It began with the breach of one commandment, "You shall not steal," a sin he never brought and confessed to Jesus. Unconfessed sin has a hardening impact on our hearts. We find that we really don't want to be close to Jesus because we don't want the light of his presence to shine on the darkness of our cherished secret sin. Ongoing sin also has the effect of opening the door of our inner lives to evil. That's exactly what happened to Judas. It was a few days later in the upper room when we read, "The devil had already put it into the heart of Judas Iscariot, Simon's son, to betray him" (John 13:2). Then we read that after Judas ate the morsel fed to him by Jesus, "Satan entered into him" (John 13:27).

This was no sudden overtaking of an otherwise innocent, devoted disciple. By indulging in evil, Judas opened the door for evil. By feeding his love of money through thievery, Judas starved any love for Jesus that might have been there.

Jesus's response to Mary's extravagant act was quite different from that of Judas. Matthew writes that Jesus said to the disciples, "Why do you trouble the woman? For she has done a beautiful thing to me" (Matt. 26:10). Mary's extravagant expression was a demonstration of how much Jesus was worth to her. Her actions expressed what she didn't have the words to express. Such extravagant love was beautiful to Jesus.

But it was more than simply beautiful to Jesus; it was meaningful to him. What Mary did had meaning beyond what most people in the room could perceive.

> Jesus said, "Leave her alone, so that she may keep it for the day of my burial. For the poor you always have with you, but you do not always have me." (John 12:7–8)

Mary, who was known for sitting at Jesus's feet, seemed to have grasped something the other disciples had so far been too thick to grasp. Immediately before Matthew's account of this supper scene, he records, "When Jesus had finished all these sayings, he said to his disciples, 'You know that after two days the Passover is coming, and the Son of Man will be delivered up to be crucified'" (Matt. 26:1–2). Jesus had been clear that he was about to die. He had even been specific enough to reveal that he was going to be crucified *at Passover*. And this was the week of Passover. Evidently most of the disciples were in denial about this. But not Mary. She had been listening. Perhaps she had put together what Jesus told her about being the resurrection and the life, along with his repeated refrain that he was about to be put to death himself. Here was Mary, the thoughtful theologian. (Don't let anyone tell you that women can't be the most astute theologians in the room!) Certainly she couldn't have seen it as clearly as we can on this side of the cross. But it seems she was able to make out that Jesus's ability to give life to others and his own death were related.

Mary broke the flask of significant worth and poured it over the body that was about to be broken, the body of one of inestimable worth. His broken body would be buried. Perhaps the fragrance of this nard would linger amid the blood and sweat. Perhaps the fragrance of Mary's devotion would linger in that enclosed tomb, the tangible scent of her confident hope in Jesus's promised resurrection. Mary had grasped the urgency of the moment and had seized the opportunity to lavish her love on Jesus while he was still with her. Cruel hands were about to take hold of him, but first her hands lovingly anointed him.

My friends, love for Jesus expressed in costly devotion is never wasted. Our most costly sacrifice could never surpass his great worth. We can never give him too much of ourselves, too much of our time, too much of our attention, too much of our affection. Jesus is worthy! In fact, in Revelation 5, we discover that it is his worthiness that we are going to sing about into eternity: "Worthy are you to take the scroll and to open its seals. . . . Worthy is the Lamb who was slain, to receive power and wealth and wisdom and might and honor and glory and blessing!" (Rev. 5:9, 12). He is worthy. He is worth it. Whatever it costs you to take hold of Jesus and enter into his death and resurrection . . . it's worth it. It won't be a waste.

In his Gospel, John seems to be inviting us to compare these two characters. He wants us to see the contrast between a person who seeks to use Jesus for personal gain and one who worships Jesus at personal loss—the contrast between a greedy person who wants to use Jesus to get the comfortable life money can buy and a grateful person who wants to honor Jesus with the best she has to give.

So let me ask you: Which person do you most identify with? Are you extravagant in your love for Jesus, demonstrating it in costly ways? For most of us, loving Jesus is rarely this kind of one-time gesture. It looks more like faithfulness week after week, diligently preparing a Sunday school lesson to teach third-graders or going out of our way to spend time with someone who needs a friend because we recognize that in loving that person, we're loving Christ. Perhaps it looks like paying the cost of losing friends because we love Christ too much to allow his name to be misused, or his loving law to be mischaracterized or his definition of what is good and beautiful to be turned upside down in our upside-down culture.

Do you see some resemblance of your devotion to Jesus in Mary's devotion? Or, if you're honest, would you have to admit that you've been hoping to use Jesus, perhaps not to make you rich, but at least to make you comfortable, to make you healthy and happy? Sometimes it seems as if Christianity is sold on these terms: come to Jesus and he will make your problems go away. Add Jesus to the life you are living to make it better. But that is not what Jesus promised, at least not for the here and now. Anyone who comes to Jesus intending to use him to get the life she wants in the here and now will ultimately discover she has not taken hold of the real Jesus.

Wasted Opportunity

Judas had become a follower of Jesus with the hope that it would be to his advantage, but now the tide seemed to be turning. Judas evidently took stock of the potential gains and losses of remaining faithful to Jesus versus the potential gains and losses if he were to align himself with Jesus's enemies. Mary's anointing of Jesus seemed to seal the deal of defection for Judas. Matthew 26:14–15 records that immediately after this dinner scene, "one of the twelve, whose name was Judas Iscariot, went to the chief priests and said, 'What will you give me if I deliver [Jesus] over to you?' And they paid him thirty pieces of silver."

It would seem Judas's motives were clear by the question he asked of the chief priests: "What will you give me . . . ?" Money was more important to Judas than Jesus. Thirty pieces of silver was all that Jesus was worth to the chief priests. Maybe Judas expected more and felt trapped by this small offer. Or maybe this was all Jesus was worth to him too.

We read in Matthew 26:16, "From that moment he sought an opportunity to betray [Jesus]." Because Judas had inside information on the habits and movements of Jesus, he would be able to arrange for the chief priests to arrest Jesus when there weren't so many people around. The chief priests knew that if they had Jesus arrested in the light of day, during this week when crowds of people were gathered in Jerusalem for Passover, there would be an uproar. They had settled on arresting Jesus after the Passover, when the crowds had gone home. But they were not ultimately in charge of their evil plot. Jesus is "the Lamb of God, who takes away the sin of the world" (John 1:29), and therefore he had to be sacrificed as the once-for-all Lamb on Passover. In other words, they might have been just trying to get rid of a threat, but in his sovereignty, God was using their evil to accomplish a far more significant purpose, the offering of his own Son as a substitutionary sacrifice for the sin of all who would put their faith in him.

> Now before the Feast of the Passover, when Jesus knew that his hour had come to depart out of this world to the Father, having loved his own who were in the world, he loved them to the end. (John 13:1)

It was the day before the Passover, and Jesus had gathered with his disciples in the upper room. But before the meal, he took off his outer garments, took up a towel, poured water into a basin, and began to work his way around the table, washing the dirty feet of his disciples. We're told that Peter was resistant to having his feet washed. He had a sense of his unworthiness. But he was not the disciple at the table who should have felt the most uncomfortable with this humble act. Judas was also there, allowing Jesus to wash his feet that had been swift to shed innocent blood.

Then we read that Jesus was troubled in his spirit and testified, "Truly, truly, I say to you, one of you will betray me" (John 13:21). Can you just imagine the disciples at this point? They must have looked around the table, zeroing in on every face, trying to figure out who it was. But there was no obvious choice. I can't imagine how Judas could have seemed on the surface to be such a devoted follower that they didn't immediately suspect him. I don't know how they missed his greed and his ambition and the hardness of his heart. But instead of asking, "Is it Judas?" they all began to ask, "Is it I, Lord?" They each saw in themselves the potential to betray the one they'd left everyone and everything to follow. And perhaps their openness to examining the genuineness of their commitment to Jesus is worthy of emulation. In fact, Paul called for it in his letter to the Corinthians, writing, "Examine yourselves, to see whether you are in the faith" (2 Cor. 13:5).

Could the most important response you have to the story of Judas be that you carve out some time for self-examination to ask yourself: "Have I truly experienced and been changed by the saving grace of Jesus Christ? Or am I just associating with other people who have done so, hoping to keep the true state of my soul hidden under a guise of following, joining, helping, but ultimately pretending?"

My husband, David, and I recently went to see *Won't You Be My Neighbor?* the documentary about *Mr. Rogers' Neighborhood.* In one poignant scene, Joyce Rogers relates a conversation with her husband, Fred Rogers, near the end of his life. She recounts that he had been reading the parable of the sheep and goats in Matthew 25, and he said to her, "Do you think I'm a sheep?" At the end of his life, as he prepared to enter into eternity, Fred Rogers was thinking deeply and honestly about the reality of his connectedness to Jesus. It is a worthy consideration for every one of us.

At one point, it was Judas who turned to Jesus and said, "Is it I, Rabbi?" and Jesus said to him, "You have said so" (Matt. 26:25). What a missed opportunity! We wish Judas would have said in that moment, "Jesus, I have something to confess. I've been stealing from the bag. I've met with the chief priests and taken money to betray you. Won't you forgive me and make me clean? When you were washing my feet everything began to shift, and I realized I don't want you to just clean my feet; I want to be clean on the inside. I'm desperate for the kind of cleansing that only you can accomplish." But Judas didn't. Sadly, Satan had launched a relentless assault on the soul of Judas that Judas didn't have the spiritual strength to withstand.

> One of his disciples, whom Jesus loved, was reclining at table at Jesus' side, so Simon Peter motioned to him to ask Jesus of whom he was speaking. So that disciple, leaning back against Jesus, said to him, "Lord, who is it?" Jesus answered, "It is he to whom I will give this morsel of bread when I have dipped it." So when he had dipped the morsel, he gave it to Judas, the son of Simon Iscariot. Then after he had taken the morsel, Satan entered into him. Jesus said to him, "What you are going to do, do quickly." Now no one at the table knew why he said this to him. Some thought that, because Judas had the moneybag, Jesus was telling him, "Buy what we need for the feast," or that he should give something to the poor. So, after receiving the morsel of bread, he immediately went out. And it was night. (John 13:23–30)

"And it was night." This, indeed, was the hour of darkness (Luke 22:53). The light that came into the world was about to be extinguished. And Judas was about to be swallowed up by the most awful darkness, the outer darkness.

Judas wasn't in the room for all that Jesus had to share with his remaining disciples in chapters 14–17 of John. He wasn't there to hear Jesus pray, "While I was with them, I kept them in your name, which you have given me. I have guarded them, and not one of them has been lost except the son of destruction, that the Scripture might be fulfilled" (John 17:12). He wasn't there to hear Jesus pray that they would be kept from the evil one (17:15). Satan had already entered into Judas through the door Judas had left open for him (Luke 22:3).

> When Jesus had spoken these words, he went out with his disciples across the brook Kidron, where there was a garden, which he and his disciples entered. Now Judas, who betrayed him, also knew the place, for Jesus often met there with his disciples. So Judas, having procured a band of soldiers and some officers from the chief priests and the Pharisees, went there with lanterns and torches and weapons. (John 18:1–3)

Knowing it would be dark in the garden and that one of the disciples might try to step forward to be arrested in place of Jesus, Judas had arranged an unmistakable sign, an intimate sign, a despicable sign considering the true nature of his intentions. He would kiss the one they were to arrest.

In his Gospel, Luke records that when Judas approached Jesus leading a crowd with swords and clubs, Jesus said to him, "Judas, would you betray the Son of Man with a kiss?" (Luke 22:48). Can you picture the twisted pain this act of treachery brought to the heart of Jesus, who had spent three years investing in Judas, walking with Judas, loving Judas? Before Judas could kiss him, Jesus had stepped forward, offering himself to those who came to arrest him. There was no need now to identify him with a kiss. Nothing would be gained by it. It would be a wasted act of wickedness.

Perhaps Jesus's question to Judas, "Would you betray the Son of Man with a kiss?" was really a final plea to Judas to separate himself from those who had set themselves against Jesus. Perhaps the question was a plea for Judas to do what the psalmist had pleaded with those who longed to be at peace with God to do: "Kiss the Son, lest he be angry" (Ps. 2:12). That would have been a kiss that saved rather than a kiss that condemned. But instead of kissing Jesus in genuine affection, Judas's kiss proved to be his final act of defection. Judas wasted his final opportunity to be genuinely joined to Jesus through repentance and faith.

Wasted Life

> When morning came, all the chief priests and the elders of the people took counsel against Jesus to put him to death. And they bound him and led him away and delivered him over to Pilate the governor.
>
> Then when Judas, his betrayer, saw that Jesus was condemned, he changed his mind and brought back the thirty pieces of silver to the chief priests and the elders, saying, "I have sinned by betraying innocent blood." They said, "What is that to us? See to it yourself." And throwing down the pieces of silver into the temple, he departed, and he went and hanged himself. But the chief priests, taking the pieces of silver, said, "It is not lawful to put them into the treasury, since it is blood money." (Matt. 27:1–6)

Evidently, when Judas saw his friend bound and condemned, the money in his pockets began to feel dirty and he became desperate to get rid of it. Evidently, Judas longed to come clean. He had closed the door to Jesus making him clean, so he went to the one source of cleansing the people in his day had been taught to count on: to the priests at the temple. But of course, the priests had blood on their hands as well. And they were not at all interested in helping Judas and his pathetic conscience. Judas was hopeless.

He seemed to be the prime example of what the writer of Hebrews would write about much later in Hebrews 6:4–6:

> For it is impossible, in the case of those who have once been enlightened [think of all the light Judas was exposed to after walking for three years with "the true light," "the light of the world," "the light of life"], who have tasted the heavenly gift [hadn't Judas tasted the bread of heaven?], and have shared in the Holy Spirit [hadn't Judas experienced the Spirit enable him to preach the word and heal the sick?], and have tasted the goodness of the word of God [hadn't Judas tasted the goodness of the words spoken by Christ, the words that give life?] and the powers of the age to come [hadn't Judas witnessed the healing powers, the resurrection powers, the restoration powers of the age to come breaking into the here and now at the behest of Jesus?], and then have fallen away, to restore them again to repentance.

Judas was an apostle who became an apostate. He abandoned the gospel. He abandoned and betrayed Christ. Surely Judas was one of the people John was referring to later in 1 John 2:19 when he wrote of those who "went out from us, but they were not of us," and then added, "If they had been of us, they would have continued with us."

The most fundamental explanation for Judas's betrayal was that his heart was untouched and unmoved by the grace of God in the person of Jesus Christ. He remained blind to the light, deaf to the word, unchanged by the powers of the age to come. He had no interest in denying himself and taking up his cross to follow Jesus.

He made his way to a piece of property he had purchased for himself—likely with money he had pilfered from the common purse. It was probably meant to be a place where he would live, enjoying the wealth he would have amassed for himself as someone in the inner circle when Jesus came to power. Instead, this piece of land became the place where he would die, taking his own life, descending into an eternity of darkness, despair, regret, and loss. What a waste.

Neither Judas's betrayal nor his suicide was the unforgivable sin. Only Judas's refusal to take hold of the grace of God in the person and work of Jesus Christ plunged him into the kind of eternity that would cause Jesus to say that it would have been better if he had never been born (Matt. 26:24). Judas didn't miss out on heaven because he was somehow destined for hell from the beginning. Judas was not moved to this act of treachery against his will. Satan entered Judas through a series of choices that Judas made that opened the door for evil to enter into his life. His relationship with Jesus was a means to an end—Judas's own comfort created by wealth. As Judas ceded more territory in his heart to the things of this world, he became increasingly resistant to Jesus and his message regarding the world to come and the riches provided there.

An Un-Wasted Death

Judas was clear enough to be able to see and say to the priests, in Matthew 27:4, "I have sinned by betraying innocent blood." He was right. In fact, he was using a technical term for his crime. Deuteronomy 27:25 forbids the shedding of innocent blood.

These priests were meant to be the mediators of mercy, and what did they say to this one so desperately seeking mercy?

> They said, "What is that to us? See to it yourself." And throwing down the pieces of silver into the temple, [Judas] departed, and he went and hanged himself. But the chief priests, taking the pieces of silver, said, "It is not lawful to put them into the treasury, since it is blood money." (Matt. 27:4–6)

What? Now they were concerned about what was not lawful? After they had arranged for the murder of the Son of God? It's hard not to laugh at the priests' unwillingness to accept back this "blood money" as "not lawful." It sounds a lot like swallowing a camel while straining a gnat, doesn't it?

The blood of Jesus was shed as a result of Judas's betrayal and the chief priests' jealousy. It was, as Judas called it, innocent blood. Never has blood been shed that was more innocent, more pure, more precious than the blood shed by Jesus. Peter wrote that we have been ransomed, "not with perishable things such as silver or gold, but with the precious blood of Christ, like that of a lamb without blemish or spot" (1 Pet. 1:18–19). Innocent blood.

But, in the sovereign plan of God, the shedding of Christ's innocent blood was not a waste! The shedding of his blood proved to be infinitely valuable, exceedingly meaningful, and completely effectual. How do we know that the innocent blood shed by Christ was not a waste? The rest of the New Testament makes it clear:

Romans 5:9: "Since, therefore, we have now been *justified by his blood*, much more shall we be saved by him from the wrath of God."

Ephesians 1:7: "In him we have *redemption through his blood*, the forgiveness of our trespasses, according to the riches of his grace."

Ephesians 2:13: "But now in Christ Jesus you who once were far off have been *brought near by the blood of Christ*."

Hebrews 9:14: "How much more will the blood of Christ, who through the eternal Spirit offered himself without blemish to God, *purify our conscience* from dead works to serve the living God."

Hebrews 13:12: "So Jesus also suffered outside the gate in order to *sanctify the people* through his own blood."

1 John 1:7: "But if we walk in the light, as he is in the light, we have fellowship with one another, and the blood of Jesus his Son *cleanses us* from all sin."

Revelation 1:5: "To him who loves us and has *freed us from our sins* by his blood."

Revelation 5:9: "And they sang a new song, saying, 'Worthy are you to take the scroll and to open its seals, for you were slain, and by your blood you *ransomed people for God* from every tribe and language and people and nation.'"

My friend, have you received the extravagant gift of this innocent blood shed on your behalf? Have you been justified by Christ's blood, redeemed through his blood, brought near by his blood? Have you had your conscience purified? Are you being sanctified, cleansed, and freed? Are you part of the people of God from every tribe and language and nation who have been ransomed by Jesus's blood? Don't be like Judas and the priests who sought to separate themselves from this blood. Come under this shed blood, value this shed blood, and accept the atoning benefit of this shed blood.

It is helpful to see the contrast in the story of Judas and Mary. But this story is not about guilting you into being as extreme as Mary in pouring out your life. It's here so that we will see the generosity of Jesus, who poured out his life. The shedding of his innocent blood is the most extravagant demonstration of love of all time. It is his extravagant love that assures us that anything we pour out in gratitude to him, in honor to him, will never be wasted.

When I survey the wondrous cross
on which the Prince of glory died,
my richest gain I count but loss,
and pour contempt on all my pride.

Forbid it, Lord, that I should boast
save in the death of Christ, my God!
All the vain things that charm me most,
I sacrifice them through his blood.

See, from his head, his hands, his feet,
sorrow and love flow mingled down.

Did e'er such love and sorrow meet,
or thorns compose so rich a crown?

Were the whole realm of nature mine,
that were a present far too small.
Love so amazing, so divine,
demands my soul, my life, my all.[17]

7

THE PRIEST

There's something amusing when a comedian impersonates a politician or celebrity in the presence of that politician or celebrity. Remember the bit on *Saturday Night Live* when Amy Poehler, portraying Hillary Clinton during her campaign for president, went into a bar, and the real Hillary Clinton was acting as the bartender? Or did you see the White House correspondent's dinner when a George W. Bush impersonator did his impression in front of the real George W. Bush? A couple of times Jimmy Fallon has dressed up as Neil Young and started singing a Neil Young song only to be joined by the real Neil Young to sing a duet.

You have the imitation face-to-face with the authentic, the impersonation face-to-face with the person.

In the biblical scene we're going to look at in this chapter, we'll witness something similar as Caiaphas, the high priest, comes face-to-face with Jesus, the Great High Priest. We'll see the shadow come face-to-face with the substance, the type stand face-to-face with the anti-type, the temporary face-to-face with the eternal, the failed face-to-face with the fulfillment. We're going to witness the scene in the Gospels when Caiaphas, the Jewish high priest in his day stood face-to-face with Jesus, the Great High Priest for all eternity.

Aaron, the First High Priest

But before we get to that key scene, let's gather some context for it. To understand the role of the high priest, we have to go back to the day when God first instructed Moses to establish the priesthood. God had rescued his people out of Egypt and brought them into his holy land, where he intended to dwell among them. But how would a holy God dwell among unholy people? There had to be a way to deal with their sin—a way for them to be cleansed of sin. This was the purpose of the entire temple system that included the tabernacle (and later the temple), the sacrifices, and the priests, who would serve as mediators between the people and God. God came down on the mountain, and he gave Moses blueprints for a tent in which he intended to come down and dwell among his people. The tent would be divided into three parts with a room at the center called the Most Holy Place. In Exodus, we read about how the tabernacle would be furnished—especially this room at the center in which God intended to dwell. Between God's presence that came down into the Most Holy Place and the ark of the covenant (a box that contained the Ten Commandment tablets) was the atonement cover, or the mercy seat. When we call this the "mercy seat," we're not talking so much about a chair but rather a location, as in "the seat of power." The atonement cover symbolized the center and source from which God showed mercy to sinners. But the atonement cover alone was not sufficient. It had to be sprinkled with the blood of a sacrifice.

God instructed Moses to appoint his brother Aaron as the first high priest. Once a year, the high priest entered into the Most Holy Place and sprinkled the blood of an animal sacrifice on the mercy seat. In this way, when God came down into the Most Holy Place, he would not, first of all, see the law that his people had broken, but instead, the blood of an atoning sacrifice.

We find chapter after chapter of detailed instructions about the priest's clothing in Exodus, then chapter after chapter in Leviticus prescribing the sacrifices to be offered and the blood to be sprinkled. That's because what happened in that room was of supreme importance. None of it was mere religiosity or ceremony for ceremony's sake. It was all about one thing: *mercy*. The high priest entered the Most Holy Place to seek mercy for himself and for God's people. He entered the room behind the curtain with the blood of a sacrifice. Blood was sprinkled on the atonement cover mediating between the perfect justice of God and the sins of the people so that they could receive mercy instead of judgment. The God who was abundant in mercy came down into the Most Holy Place to extend mercy to his people—and all of it mediated by the high priest.

When we meet people, and we ask what line of work they are in, sometimes they will talk in more general terms of the business they're in rather than their specific jobs. A nurse might say she is in the health care business. A teacher might say she works in education. If Aaron or his sons had been asked, "What do you do?" their answer could have been, "I'm in the mercy business. I mediate and deliver the mercy of God to sinful people. I represent sinful people before a holy God in such a way that they can expect God's mercy instead of his wrath."

This was particularly the case one day a year, when the high priest would enter into the Most Holy Place. We read about it in Leviticus 16.

> And the LORD said to Moses, "Tell Aaron your brother not to come at any time into the Holy Place inside the veil, before the mercy seat that is on the ark, so that he may not die. For I will appear in the cloud over the mercy seat." (Lev. 16:2)

Aaron couldn't just go into the Most Holy Place any time he wanted. He could enter it only one day a year.

> And he shall take from the congregation of the people of Israel two male goats for a sin offering, and one ram for a burnt offering.

> Aaron shall offer the bull as a sin offering for himself and shall make atonement for himself and for his house. (Lev. 16:5–6)

To enter into God's holy presence, the high priest had to be ceremonially cleansed of his own sin. So after washing, he offered a bull as a sin offering for himself. Then two goats were brought to him.

> And Aaron shall cast lots over the two goats, one lot for the LORD and the other lot for Azazel. And Aaron shall present the goat on which the lot fell for the LORD and use it as a sin offering, but the goat on which the lot fell for Azazel shall be presented alive before the LORD to make atonement over it, that it may be sent away into the wilderness to Azazel. (Lev. 16:8–10)

When the people saw the high priest slit the throat of the first goat and carry its blood behind the curtain, they would have thought, *That should be my blood. That is what my sin deserves. But God has allowed the death sentence I deserve to be passed onto this animal instead of me. Death for the substitute; mercy for me.*

Then the high priest would put his hands on the second goat's head and begin to confess the sins of the people, ceremonially transferring their guilt to the goat. As the priest worked his way through their specific sins—their lack of love for God, their cruelty toward each other, their coveting, their lying, their adultery—the people would have heard their own sins spoken by the priest. Then they would have watched as the goat was led away through the sea of tents, outside the camp, and into the wilderness, never to be seen again, and they would have felt relief that their sin-guilt had been carried far away. "Death for the scapegoat; mercy for me."

What is important for us to understand is that their system of priests and tabernacle and temple and sacrifices was always intended to be a pointer toward something more significant. It was preparation, an object lesson, an illustration of how it would be possible for sinners to receive mercy that would enable not just the priest, but all of God's people to enter into God's holy presence. And not just once a year but all the time. Every high priest who ever entered behind the curtain of the Most Holy Place was there to serve as a shadow of a greater high priest to come. Every sacrifice offered was a shadow of the once-for-all perfect sacrifice to be provided. The Most Holy Place itself was, as Hebrews 8:5 calls it, "a copy and shadow" of the heavenly things.

As we read about all the detailed instructions for priests and their clothing and their sacrifices and the account of God's glory coming down to dwell in the Most Holy Place in Exodus, it would make sense that we would have high hopes for how these priests would serve to mediate the mercy of God to his people. But from the very outset, the Aaronic priesthood was shown to be inadequate. It was like a newly christened ship that sank the moment it hit the water. When Moses lingered longer than expected on Mount Sinai meeting with God, Aaron, the first high priest, led the people of God in throwing their gold into a fire to make a golden calf (Ex. 32:2). Later, we read about Aaron's sons, who decided not to follow God's clear instructions on how to offer sacrifice and did it their own way, and were consumed by fire (Lev. 10:1–2).

The sad reality was that none of Israel's high priests ever lived up to what God intended for those he had set apart to serve him in his temple. In 2 Chronicles 36:14, we read that "all the officers of the priests and the people likewise were exceedingly unfaithful, following all the abominations of the nations. And they polluted the house of the LORD that he had made holy in Jerusalem." As we read through the history of Israel in the Old Testament, we discover that, as much as anything else, it was the corruption of the priests that caused Israel to be judged by God in the form of exile to Babylon.

The Lord, however, did not abandon the priesthood. Instead, he pledged to restore it after the exile. As the people were in exile in Babylon, Jeremiah recorded God's promise that David's sons would again sit on Israel's throne (kingship) and that Levi's sons would again offer sacrifices for the nation (priesthood) (Jer. 33:17–18). In fact, when the Jews returned to Jerusalem after their exile in Babylon, the high priesthood was reinstated. Joshua, the son of Jehozadak, was high priest in the time of Haggai and Zechariah (Hag. 2:2–4). The list of sons who followed him in his high priestly role is found in Nehemiah 12. But as centuries went by, the office of high priest began to change. Foreign powers came to power over the Jewish people and began appointing the high priests. They were no longer chosen based on being descendants of Aaron but based on who was willing to pay, cooperate, and exercise power in a way that pleased the foreign rulers. The role of high priest became a mixture of religion and politics. In other words, instead of the role of high priest being about extending mercy from God, it became all about exercising power over the people.

Caiaphas, the Last High Priest

Josephus, a Jewish historian, tells us that when the Romans took direct control of Judea in AD 6, Anas was the first high priest they appointed. He served ten years, followed briefly by his son. Then his son-in-law, Caiaphas, was appointed, who served about eighteen years. Josephus claims that Caiaphas bought his place in the priesthood by paying Herod a sum of money. If we want to think of the timing in relation to the life of Jesus, we could say that Anas was appointed when Jesus was a boy, and then Caiaphas served as high priest when Jesus was a teen until after his death.

As priests, Anas and Caiaphas were far more interested in political power than in priestly piety. Caiaphas must have been good at keeping the peace because he held the office for a very long time compared to most high priests in that era. Then a man from Galilee stepped onto the scene. He was a carpenter from Nazareth, but he taught with authority. He spoke of a kingdom that was not of this world. He was doing miracles that had all the people talking. He pointed to himself as the way into the good graces of God. Instead of supporting the temple system they had set up, he was overturning tables in the temple. He was a threat to the priests' power and position. The people had wanted to seize him and make him their king, but he slipped away. What if he let them crown him king the next time they tried? What if Rome found out the high priests were losing control of the people? The powers of Rome might just step in and take away the priests' power and position. The Romans might demolish the temple and put an end to everything about their way of life. Something had to be done.

His Plot

And then the religious leaders heard about Lazarus. Earlier Jesus had raised a little girl to life, but it was right after she had died, so while it had been big news, it was not as big as Lazarus. This time, Jesus had raised someone from the dead who had been in the tomb for *four days*. This was the last straw. "So the chief priests and the Pharisees gathered the council and said, 'What are we to do? For this man performs many signs. If we let him go on like this, everyone will believe in him, and the Romans will come and take away both our place and our nation'" (John 11:47–48).

Who is this council? The Sanhedrin was a little bit like the Supreme Court and Congress rolled into one. It was comprised of seventy-one priests, scribes, and elders, and the high priest presided over it. The chief priests that were part of this group were drawn from the extended family of the high priest. They were not really into mercy; they were into control. Their concern was less about the well-being of the people than about the preservation of their own power and prestige. They thought that if they put Jesus to death, things would quiet down.

His Prophetic Words

Caiaphas, the high priest—a seasoned political veteran—announced what he saw as the most politically expedient solution. "But one of

them, Caiaphas, who was high priest that year, said to them, 'You
know nothing at all. Nor do you understand that it is better for you
that one man should die for the people, not that the whole nation
should perish'" (John 11:49–50).

"You know nothing at all . . . you're really naïve," he was saying
to the group. "Let's find a quiet, acceptable way to make a scapegoat of Jesus." It all sounded so reasonable, when really it was
criminal. It sounded pragmatic, when really it was prophetic.

Caiaphas was not intending to be prophetic. He was merely
stating what seemed like a reasonable plan. He didn't realize that
he was articulating the most profound truth in the universe. John,
the Gospel writer, made that clear when he added:

> He did not say this of his own accord, but being high priest
> that year he prophesied that Jesus would die for the nation,
> and not for the nation only, but also to gather into one the
> children of God who are scattered abroad. So from that day on
> they made plans to put him to death. (John 11:51–53)

When John wrote that Caiaphas "did not say this on his own,"
he didn't mean that God was using Caiaphas like a puppet. Caiaphas said exactly what he intended to say. But when he spoke, God
was also speaking. What Caiaphas intended to communicate was
the human perspective about the purpose of the death of Jesus.
Unknowingly, he also communicated the divine perspective about
what the death of Jesus would accomplish. Caiaphas was merely
making a human plan, but God, in his sovereignty, intended to use
this evil plan to accomplish the greatest good of all time. God used
this human plan to carry out his divine plan.

To understand this, let's look more closely at Caiaphas's statement, "It is better for you that one man should die for the people,
not that the whole nation should perish."

"It is better for you." Who was "you," and how would it be "better"? "You" for Caiaphas was the council. Maintaining power was
his first concern. The council was more likely to maintain its

power if Jesus died and the Romans saw that the ruling council had dealt with a potential uprising by the people who wanted to make Jesus their king instead of Caesar. It would be better for the ruling council.

What did Caiaphas mean when he said that one man should die "for the people"? Caiaphas meant "for the benefit of the people." But in reality, this one man, Jesus, would die "in the place of" the people. Caiaphas, the high priest, the one who every year took the head of a goat into his hands and slit its throat so that the people wouldn't have to die. The goat died "for" or "in the place of" the people. Caiaphas, the one who every year put his hands on the head of another goat and confessed the sins of the people and sent it out into the wilderness as a scapegoat in order to spare the people. And he missed the irony. Caiaphas missed the reality that God had always intended to provide a once-for-all perfect sacrifice that all the sacrifices offered by high priests throughout the centuries had been pointing toward. The longtime high priest missed the reality that Jesus was *the* sacrifice, *the* scapegoat, who would carry away the sins of "the people."

Who were "the people"? To Caiaphas, "the people" were national and political Israel. John pointed out the erroneous limitation of Caiaphas's words in verse 52, explaining that Jesus would not just die for "the nation" but would "gather into one the children of God who are scattered abroad." Throughout John's Gospel, the "children of God" are defined as those who believe on or in Jesus. Jesus had spoken of this "gathering into one" earlier. Back in John 10, we read that Jesus said,

> I am the good shepherd. I know my own and my own know me, just as the Father knows me and I know the Father; and I lay down my life for the sheep. And I have other sheep that are not of this fold. I must bring them also, and they will listen to my voice. So there will be one flock, one shepherd. (John 10:14–16)

The death of Christ was the means by which all God's scattered children would be gathered into this one flock. Without realizing it, Caiaphas prophesied that the death of Jesus would result in the gathering of a people from every tribe, tongue, and nation.

And here is where this story becomes personal to each one of us. Perhaps the most significant question each of us must ask ourselves is whether or not we are included in "the people"; if we have been gathered into this one flock by this one, good shepherd.

There is one more significant word in Caiaphas's short statement. He said that it would be better that one man die for the people than that the whole nation "perish." Of course, what Caiaphas had in mind when he spoke of perishing was the temporal destruction of the nation of Israel. But once again, he was saying more than he realized. He was so very shortsighted, while God's intentions for his words were so far-reaching. The death of this one man, Jesus, would not, in fact, keep the religious leaders and the temple in Jerusalem from perishing. In less than forty years, the temple and its priesthood would be destroyed. It all would perish. But the death of this one man would have saving, protecting power. All who took hold of this one man by faith would not perish, or, as John put it earlier in his Gospel, "whoever believes in him should not perish but have eternal life" (John 3:16).

So we've heard how Caiaphas used his influence as high priest over Israel to lead them down a path of crucifying the promised Savior. Imagine if Caiaphas had said what someone who held this divinely prescribed office should have said: "Gentlemen, this Jesus of Nazareth, who just raised Lazarus, must be the Christ, sent from God. Let's repent of all our resistance to him and hatred for him, and believe in him. We don't need to be afraid of the Romans or of losing the temple. If Jesus has just raised a man from the dead, surely he can protect us from the Romans. If he is the Christ, he will fulfill everything that the temple, the sacrifices, and the priesthood were meant to be in such a way that not only will we not perish, but the life we gain with him will be everything God has intended for his people—people from every tribe, tongue, and nation—since the very beginning."

Of course, that was not what Caiaphas said. The plot of the Sanhedrin was hatched. They were just looking for opportunity to carry it out. And we know from our previous chapter on Judas how the opportunity presented itself. Judas offered to provide insider information on where they could arrest Jesus in the dark of night outside the city where there would be no riot.

We'll turn to Matthew's account to see what happened when Jesus came face-to-face with Caiaphas.

His Prophetic False Testimony

> Then those who had seized Jesus led him to Caiaphas the high priest, where the scribes and the elders had gathered. And Peter was following him at a distance, as far as the courtyard of the high priest, and going inside he sat with the guards to see the end. Now the chief priests and the whole council were seeking false testimony against Jesus that they might put him to death, but they found none, though many false witnesses came forward. (Matt. 26:57–60)

Here we have it. The substance stood before shadow, the authentic before imposter. Caiaphas and the rest of the council had been trying to find someone who would give false testimony. If anyone had ever thought the council was interested in obedience to God's law, the truth was clear. It was clear that the Sanhedrin was failing to uphold the ninth commandment, "You shall not bear false witness" (Ex. 20:16). They found two people who were willing to take something Jesus said and twist it into an offense they could take to the Roman court, where the death penalty could be enacted.

> At last two came forward and said, "This man said, 'I am able to destroy the temple of God, and to rebuild it in three days.'" (Matt. 26:60–61)

These two witnesses must have been in the temple when Jesus was overturning the tables and heard him say, "Destroy this temple, and in three days I will raise it up" (John 2:19). They perceived that he was intending to somehow knock down the stones and pillars of Herod's Temple. But Jesus wasn't threatening to destroy the temple; he was anticipating the destruction of the true temple, his own body, in the crucifixion (John 2:21). Just as it was substance before shadow when Jesus stood before the high priest, so it was substance in shadow when Jesus entered into the temple. Jesus was everything the temple had been built to point toward. Jesus, in himself, was the true temple, the place where sinners experience mercy from a just God.

But in this false testimony, Caiaphas found something he could work with, a Roman law he could frame Jesus for breaking. Desecrating a holy place would have been viewed as a capital offense to the Romans, so if Jesus had threatened to destroy Jerusalem's temple, Caiaphas had something.

His Prophetic Confusion

> But Jesus remained silent. And the high priest said to him, "I adjure you by the living God, tell us if you are the Christ, the Son of God." (Matt. 26:63)

Caiaphas wanted to know if Jesus was claiming to be the Christ, the Messiah. Why wouldn't Jesus answer the question directly? Why not say, "Yes, that's me. I am the Christ"? What Caiaphas and the Jewish people meant when they spoke of the Messiah was so very different from what Jesus came to be and do. The Jews expected the Messiah to be a nationalistic military liberator, and Jesus had no intentions of that. So Jesus simply wouldn't answer the question on Caiaphas's terms.

Caiaphas was pushing. There was only one truth-teller in the room, and Caiaphas had the gall to ask him to swear by an oath. That's what he was doing when he said, "I adjure you by the living God." Of course, the truth that Jesus had to tell was more than Caiaphas could bear.

> Jesus said to him, "You have said so. But I tell you, from now on you will see the Son of Man seated at the right hand of Power and coming on the clouds of heaven." (Matt. 26:64)

Jesus wouldn't define himself on Caiaphas's terms, but he would define himself in the terms used by David in Psalm 110 and Daniel in Daniel 7. In Psalm 110, David wrote about a heavenly conversation he overheard:

> The LORD says to my Lord:
> "Sit at my right hand,
> until I make your enemies your footstool." (Ps. 110:1)

By alluding to Psalm 110, Jesus was telling Caiaphas that he was the eternal Son who was told by God the Father that he would sit at his right hand.

In Daniel 7:13, Daniel wrote:

> I saw in the night visions,
> and behold, with the clouds of heaven
>   there came one like a son of man,
> and he came to the Ancient of Days
>   and was presented before him.

By alluding to Daniel 7, Jesus was saying that he was the Son of Man that Caiaphas would one day see coming with the clouds of heaven. Caiaphas might have been standing before Jesus as judge on that night, but that night would soon be past, and Caiaphas would see who was really the judge. Caiaphas, the earthly judge, was standing face-to-face with the ultimate Judge. Caiaphas may have thought of himself as having had all the power in that moment, but Jesus was making it clear that Caiaphas was going to see who really had all the power. If you look in your Bible at Matthew 26:64, you'll probably see that the word "Power" is capitalized.

This was not power in the abstract but Power as a person, the almighty God. Jesus was claiming to have all the power of almighty God as the Son who sits at his right hand.

Jesus may have been standing before Caiaphas bound as a prisoner, but the next time Caiaphas would see him, Jesus would be seated on the divine throne of glory. Implied in his declaration was that Caiaphas and the rest of this corrupt council would one day have to give an account for what they had conspired to do to this one who, in Caiaphas's own words, was "the Christ, the Son of God" (v. 63).

By using this Old Testament title and allusion, Jesus was telling Caiaphas that he was the Son of Man before whom all kingdoms would eventually bow, whose dominion would be everlasting and indestructible. He was the Son of David who was also David's Lord. He was the one whom God would vindicate, who would sit at God's right hand, and with whom God would share his throne. That was how Caiaphas should think of him. From this time forward, Jesus was saying to Caiaphas, "There is only my kingdom, my rule, my glory. That's it." No wonder it made Caiaphas so mad that he tore his clothes.

His Prophetic Act

> Then the high priest tore his robes and said, "He has uttered blasphemy. What further witnesses do we need? You have now heard his blasphemy. What is your judgment?" They answered, "He deserves death." (Matt. 26:65–66)

The judges in a Jewish trial for blasphemy were bound to rend their clothes when blasphemous words were uttered, and those clothes were never to be mended. So this act was a formal sign of condemnation. Caiaphas rent his garments in mock holy horror because Jesus had confirmed the truth that he was the Christ, the Son of the living God. And yet, in tearing his clothes, perhaps Caiaphas was again communicating something more than he realized. By tearing his robes, he surely did not intend to communicate an end to the office of the high priesthood in Israel, but in fact, that was what was happening.

Once again, we have to imagine how this could have been different. Here was the high priest of Israel. His whole life should have been given over to helping God's people look for and welcome God's great prophet, priest, and king. Instead, Caiaphas was conspiring to crucify God's King. He should have been invested in helping God's people see their need for a greater temple, a greater sacrifice, and, in fact, a greater high priest. As the high priest of Israel, Caiaphas's heart should have burned with a longing to see the Christ. But instead his heart burned to destroy the Christ. As the high priest, he should have led the people in rending their garments in repentance before the Holy One instead of rending his own garment in rage against the Holy One.

Standing there before Caiaphas was the one who came to deliver, bound in chains. The righteous judge was condemned by a corrupt court. The prince of glory was spat upon and struck and slapped in a shameful display of defiance. The Resurrection and the Life was sentenced to die.

Rather than tear his high priestly garment, Caiaphas should have removed it and given it to the Great High Priest who stood before him. He should have said, "The days of having a high priest in Israel are now over, now that the Great High Priest has come. He will lead all God's people into the very presence of God. No longer should anyone come to me seeking mercy. Instead, as one who is in desperate need of mercy myself, I'm turning toward the only one who can truly mediate the mercy of God to undeserving sinners."

It was only a few hours later when "Jesus cried out again with a loud voice and yielded up his spirit. And behold, the curtain of the temple was torn in two" (Matt. 27:50–51).

Perhaps it was a divine response to Caiaphas, who tore his robes in a twisted display of grief. Perhaps it was as if God, the one who had once dwelt among his people in the Most Holy Place, tore his own robe—the curtain that surrounded him—in agony as his Son breathed his last.

Jesus, the Great High Priest

The death of Jesus was the end of the priesthood. Even though there actually were a couple more high priests in Jerusalem before the temple was destroyed in AD 70, Caiaphas was the last high priest to serve as a pointer to the Great High Priest, Jesus. There was simply no need for an imperfect priest once the perfect priest had come. "And since we have a great priest over the house of God, let us draw near with a true heart in full assurance of faith, with our hearts sprinkled clean from an evil conscience and our bodies washed with pure water" (Heb. 10:21–23). Based on the kind of high priest we have, the most reasonable response should be to draw near to God.

The death of Jesus was the end of the sacrificial system. No more innocent lambs needed to be slain. "He did this once for all when he offered up himself" (Heb. 7:27).

The death of Jesus was the end of the temple made with limestone in Jerusalem. But it was not the end of all the temple was meant to be. When the True Temple was destroyed, sure enough, it was raised in three days. Jesus was raised from the dead, he ascended into heaven, and then forty days later the fire of God in the person of the Holy Spirit descended not over the Most Holy Place of the temple in Jerusalem, but over the heads of believers gathered in an upper room as they waited and prayed for power. They became living, breathing temples of the Holy Spirit, living stones that were "being built up as a spiritual house, to be a holy priesthood, to offer spiritual sacrifices acceptable to God through Jesus Christ" (1 Pet. 2:5).

The death of Jesus was the fulfillment of the Day of Atonement. No longer was there a need for a high priest to slit the throat of a goat and sprinkle its blood on the veil. The veil was split. Jesus "entered once for all into the holy places, not by means of the blood of goats and calves but by means of his own blood, thus securing an eternal redemption" (Heb. 9:12). No longer was there a need for the high priest to confess sins onto the head of the other goat, the scapegoat, and send him out into the wilderness to die. All the sins of God's people were laid upon the one true scapegoat. At the cross, "the LORD has laid on him the iniquity of us all" (Isa. 53:6), so that we might know: "as far as the east is from the west, so far does he remove our transgressions from us" (Ps. 103:12).

The death of Jesus was the end of once-a-year access into the presence of God by one high priest. The tearing of the veil in essence threw open the door. Because the sins of all those who put their trust in Christ are fully dealt with in the death of Jesus, forgiven sinners are now welcomed into the presence of God in union with Christ. "We have confidence to enter the holy places by the blood of Jesus, by the new and living way that he opened for us through the curtain, that is, through his flesh" (Heb. 10:19–21). The tearing of the curtain was a tangible sign of the tearing of Christ's flesh. Because his flesh was torn, we can enter in.

Have you? Have you entered in? And if not, why not? Could it be that you don't see yourself in need of mercy? Or is it that you don't really believe you will receive mercy?

Poor Caiaphas. He didn't see himself in need of mercy, and therefore he never cried out for it. No wonder he was unfit for the role of high priest, the role of extending and inviting God's people into experiencing the generosity of God's mercy. My friend, if you don't see yourself in need of mercy, I pray that God will open your eyes to the reality of your own soul, that you will see its deadness, its darkness. I pray that instead of the reality of your sin making you hopeless, it will make you determined to reach out to the only source of the mercy you need.

And if you are someone who doesn't really believe that you will receive mercy, I pray that God will open your eyes to the kindness and generosity of your Great High Priest who loves to lavish mercy on people who don't deserve it.

Someday you are going to stand before the Judge of all the earth. He won't be a wicked, corrupt judge like Caiaphas. He will be the perfect judge, Jesus himself. All who cry out to him for mercy now will stand before him not only as their judge, but as their Advocate, as their Great High Priest. All who cry out to him find mercy today and will still be experiencing his mercy on that great day and into eternity.

> For we do not have a high priest who is unable to sympathize with our weaknesses, but one who in every respect has been tempted as we are, yet without sin. Let us then with confidence draw near to the throne of grace, that we may receive mercy and find grace to help in time of need. (Heb. 4:15–16)

Before the throne of God above
I have a strong and perfect plea,
A great High Priest whose name is Love
Who ever lives and pleads for me.
My name is graven on His hands,
My name is written on His heart;
I know that while in heav'n He stands
No tongue can bid me thence depart.[18]

8

THE CRIMINALS

Can I tell you the three words I love to hear more than any others? I love it when someone says to me, "You were right." My brilliance and insight are proven and recognized. What a sense of satisfaction.

But closely connected to these three words I love are three words I despise. Three words I find very, very hard to spit out are: "I was wrong." I want to explain. I want to excuse. I want to hide from it, avoid it, and deny it. Not only do these words knock me down a notch, they sometimes make me responsible for making things right where I have been wrong. And usually that costs me something—something I don't want to pay.

As humans, we have an amazing ability to deny our very real culpability, don't we? And of course, we live in a society in which we're always being told that we shouldn't feel guilty, that guilt—whether or not it is warranted—is a useless, harmful emotion that should be jettisoned.

Perhaps that's what makes some of the response we've seen to the #MeToo movement so interesting. At one point, as women began to take to social media, using the hashtag #MeToo to tell the world about how they had been sexually harassed, assaulted, or abused, another hashtag emerged: #ItWasMe. As the bad behavior of media moguls, television stars, business executives, and even religious leaders began to come to light, it prompted many men to begin to examine their own history for something ugly that they had never before seen in themselves.

In October of 2017, *Elite Daily*, an online newsmagazine, published a story titled, "#ItWasMe Is the Hashtag for Men Who Are Taking Responsibility for Rape Culture."[19] In the story, a man named Kyle Misner is quoted saying that when the #MeToo posts started populating his timeline, it got him thinking about his own past and whether he was someone else's #MeToo. One particular instance sprung to his mind: "I said, in my head, 'That was sexual assault.' It was a hard thing to admit to myself to realize I had assaulted someone. Over the course of the day, I went over other things in my past trying to see what else I was either guilty of or complicit about." That period of self-examination led to him to later tweet:

> #itwasme in my early twenties when I touched my very first partner inappropriately while she slept next to me.
> #itwasme at 12/13 when my cousin and I lightly kissed a girl who fell asleep in the living room while we were watching TV.
> #itwasme as a teenager in high school when I would stare and zone out at girls, certainly creeping them out.
> #itwasme in high school when a classmate mentioned fantasizing about rape and I remained silent.
> #itwasme when I would laugh with others and/or joke about such things as "if there's grass on the field, play ball" or "any port in a storm." This is one example of the **** that people mean when they talk about rape culture.
> #itwasme No matter how much good I've done, or how much better I am or strive to be now, it doesn't erase the past. I'm not proud of these things but I own my contributions to #metoo.[19]

I admire the courage it takes to explore, confess, and come clean regarding what would be more convenient to excuse, ignore, and forget, don't you? It takes a lot of courage to admit, "I was wrong. I'm guilty. It was me."

I admire it in other people. But I find I don't like doing it myself. Yet, this is what the gospel calls us to every day. It calls us to take an unflinching look at what we would like to excuse, ignore, and forget, and to be willing to say, "I'm guilty. I've been wrong." It also assures us that when we do, we will be met with mercy and grace. We have a standing invitation to confess and come clean before the only truly innocent person who has ever lived. He never had anything to confess, he never had any dark secret, he never had any uncleanness of his own. Yet he was proclaimed guilty and condemned to death.

Jesus, the Righteous Man

The contrast of innocence and guilt seems to have been heavy on Luke's mind as he penned his account of the death of Jesus in his Gospel. He seems to want to make sure his readers see the complete innocence of Jesus in dramatic contrast to the guilt of those who surrounded him. Notice the contrast in this scene found in Luke 23:

> Pilate then called together the chief priests and the rulers and the people, and said to them, "You brought me this man as one who was misleading the people. And after examining him before you, behold, *I did not find this man guilty* of any of your charges against him. Neither did Herod, for he sent him back to us. Look, *nothing deserving death has been done by him.* I will therefore punish and release him."
>
> But they all cried out together, "Away with this man, and release to us Barabbas"—a man who had been thrown into prison for an insurrection started in the city and for murder. Pilate addressed them once more, desiring to release Jesus, but they kept shouting, "Crucify, crucify him!" A third time he said to them, "Why? What evil has he done? *I have found in him no guilt* deserving death. I will therefore punish and release

him." But they were urgent, demanding with loud cries that he should be crucified. And their voices prevailed. So Pilate decided that their demand should be granted. He released the man who had been thrown into prison for insurrection and murder, for whom they asked, but he delivered Jesus over to their will. (Luke 23:13–25)

Three times in this brief scene Pilate makes his finding clear— "I find no guilt in this man"; "I did not find this man guilty"; "Nothing deserving death has been done by him." In his account of this scene, Matthew adds another voice asserting the innocence of Jesus, that of Pilate's wife, who sent word to Pilate saying, "Have nothing to do with *that righteous man*, for I have suffered much because of him today in a dream" (Matt. 27:19). Ironically, Pilate's wife was the only person in the course of several trials whose testimony about Jesus was truthful. Jesus was not only innocent of blasphemy, treason, evading taxes, and inciting a revolt; he was completely and utterly innocent of all wrong.

But the same cannot be said of Barabbas.

The Notorious Prisoner

Barabbas, according to Matthew, was a notorious prisoner (Matt. 27:15). Mark adds that he was "among the rebels in prison, who had committed murder in the insurrection" (Mark 15:7). Today we would probably call him a terrorist. He had had it with Roman rule, with their unfair taxes and their corrupt, oppressive government; and evidently, he did not care about the Jews who had become collateral damage in his rebellion against Rome.

We could think of his name this way: *bar*, which means "son of," and *abbas*, which means "father." So his name means "son of the father." Surely he was named this way in reference to the father who raised him. But the rebellion at the heart of his crime indicates that in a far deeper way, he was clearly the son of his father, Adam. He was a rebel against Rome, and ultimately against

God. He had no interest in submitting to either of their laws. One would think that Barabbas would have been the last person the people in Jerusalem would want to see released from prison. He was dangerous. He was a hardened, callous criminal. He deserved to die for his crimes. To release him would have been a great injustice.

So why would Pilate have even suggested that Barabbas be released? This was the week of Passover, the most important religious feast of the year for the Jews. It was the time when they remembered that they were prisoners in Egypt, which also made it the perfect time for the Roman ruler to curry a little favor among them by releasing a prisoner. It gave him the appearance of being sympathetic to their history and accommodating to their religion.

This particular Passover, Pilate had a notorious prisoner to offer—Barabbas. Pilate was quite certain that the crowds would not want this terrorist released, and that, surely, they would want him to grant amnesty to this other prisoner, Jesus, who had clearly done no wrong.

But Pilate severely underestimated the will of the people. Matthew tells us, "Now the chief priests and the elders persuaded the crowd to ask for Barabbas and destroy Jesus" (Matt. 27:20). Luke tells us, "They were urgent, demanding with loud cries that he should be crucified. And their voices prevailed" (Luke 23:23).

> The governor again said to them, "Which of the two do you want me to release for you?" And they said, "Barabbas." Pilate said to them, "Then what shall I do with Jesus who is called Christ?" They all said, "Let him be crucified!" And he said, "Why? What evil has he done?" But they shouted all the more, "Let him be crucified!" (Matt. 27:21–23)

Understand what was happening here. Jesus was the true "Son of the Father." The Father had sent him to his people to call them to himself, and they had utterly rejected Jesus. We can't help but think again of the parable Jesus told about the vineyard owner

155

who sent a series of servants to his tenants to get his fruit harvest. But the tenants took his servants and beat one, killed another, and stoned another. So the vineyard owner sent his son, but the tenants threw him out of the vineyard and killed him too. That's exactly what was happening. The crowds of people in Jerusalem were calling out for Barabbas, "son of the father," to be released, and for the one who was truly the Son of the Father to be executed.

The Bloodguilty Crowd

If we're looking for guilty parties in this scene, we can point to the religious leaders who accused Jesus, or to Pilate who allowed this miscarriage of justice, or even the very guilty Barabbas. But the crowds of people in Jerusalem that day share the burden of guilt. In fact, according to Matthew's account of the scene, they were more than happy to bear the guilt of condemning Jesus to death:

> So when Pilate saw that he was gaining nothing, but rather that a riot was beginning, he took water and washed his hands before the crowd, saying, "I am innocent of this man's blood; see to it yourselves." And all the people answered, "His blood be on us and on our children!" (Matt. 27:24–25)

Their hearts were so hard toward Jesus that they called down a curse on themselves to urge Pilate to act. When the people said, "His blood be on us," their words carried a huge weight of Old Testament seriousness. To shed innocent blood was the worst category of sin in the Mosaic Law. It was this sin that David asked God to cleanse him of in Psalm 51 when he said, "Deliver me from bloodguiltiness, O God" (Ps. 51:14) after he had arranged for the murder of innocent Uriah. The prophet Jeremiah called down destruction on Jerusalem "because they have filled this place with the blood of innocents," burning their sons in the fire as burnt offerings to Baal (Jer. 19:4–5). The crowd's hatred for Jesus burned so strong that they were willing to be cut off from all God's promises to bless and to receive God's curse instead, if only Pilate would put Jesus to death.

Innocent, unblemished lambs had been herded into Jerusalem all that week. The Jews had taken these lambs into their homes to be slain for the Passover. The blood of these lambs should have reminded them of that night in Egypt when the blood of an unblemished lamb was painted on the doorframes of their houses to protect their families from judgment. In the first Passover, safety and salvation were found under the covering of the blood of the lamb. And so it was on this day. The people had the opportunity to come under the blood of Christ in faith and find salvation, but instead they cried out for his innocent blood to come down on them in judgment. Instead of receiving him, they rejected him.

> There is a fountain filled with blood,
> Drawn from Immanuel's veins,
> And sinners plunged beneath that flood
> Lose all their guilty stains:
> Lose all their guilty stains,
> Lose all their guilty stains;
> And sinners plunged beneath that flood
> Lose all their guilty stains.[20]

Then [Pilate] released for them Barabbas, and having scourged Jesus, delivered him to be crucified. (Matt. 27:26)

A cross had been prepared for Barabbas. He had been found guilty and condemned to death for his crimes. But someone took his place. Someone who was perfectly innocent took the place of Barabbas on that cross, and Barabbas was set free.

> Bearing shame and scoffing rude,
> In my place condemned He stood;
> Sealed my pardon with His blood.
> Hallelujah! What a Savior![21]

Barabbas was the first person in history who could sing these words, but he was not the last! Barabbas was not the only guilty person saved from death through the death of the innocent Christ. All who are joined to Jesus Christ by faith can say, "I am guilty. It was me. But someone has been punished in my place so that I can be set free." We can say, "For our sake [God] made him to be sin who knew no sin, so that in him we might become the righteousness of God" (2 Cor. 5:21). This is the too-good-to-be-trueness of the gospel.

The Scoffers and Mockers

Just as Luke seemed to want his readers to see the innocence of Jesus in contrast to the guilt of those around him, he also seemed to want his readers to see the similarities between the temptation of Jesus during this crucifixion scene and the temptation Jesus experienced in the wilderness at the very beginning of his ministry. Remember that in the wilderness, Satan said to Jesus three times, "If you are the Son of God . . ." followed by a temptation for Jesus to avoid suffering and take care of himself. The agents of Satan in this crucifixion scene did something similar. In fact, three times they implored Jesus to save himself—first the religious rulers, then the soldiers, and finally one of the robbers who was being crucified alongside him.

> And the people stood by, watching, but the rulers scoffed at him, saying, "He saved others; *let him save himself,* if he is the Christ of God, his Chosen One!" The soldiers also mocked him, coming up and offering him sour wine and saying, "If you are the King of the Jews, *save yourself!*" There was also an inscription over him, "This is the King of the Jews."
>
> One of the criminals who were hanged railed at him, saying, "Are you not the Christ? *Save yourself* and us!" (Luke 23:35–39)

They all taunted Jesus with the words "Save yourself," though they all meant it in different ways. The religious rulers actually admitted that Jesus had "saved others." They could not deny his healing and feeding miracles or the fact that he had raised Lazarus from the dead. But they could not accept that these miraculous powers came from God, or that they pointed to the truth that Jesus was the one whom God promised to send.

The Roman soldiers challenged Jesus to save himself in the context of being a king. He had a sign over his head that said "King of the Jews." Of course, Pilate put it there to make a joke out of Jesus. What kind of king has thorns for a crown, a cross for a throne, and no standing army to fight for him? Twelve legions of angels were ready to come at Christ's command, but this army could not be seen by the Roman soldiers.

Then there was the criminal on the neighboring cross who must have been struggling for his every breath at this point, yet he used some of that precious breath to breathe out his disdain for Jesus. He had heard Jesus pray for forgiveness for his enemies. Of course, to this man, that was just further proof that Jesus was no real messiah. He was too soft, too weak. This criminal and his band wanted a Messiah who would crush their enemies not pray for their enemies. And from where he hung, Jesus couldn't even seem to save himself from a Roman cross.

They all implored Jesus to save himself. And of course, he could have saved himself! But if he had, he could not have saved us.

> But he was pierced for our transgressions;
>> he was crushed for our iniquities;
> upon him was the chastisement that brought us peace,
>> and with his wounds we are healed. (Isa. 53:5)

By choosing not to save himself, Jesus opened up a way of salvation that at least one person in this scene embraced.

The Dying Thief

Likely, the two thieves that were hung on either side of Jesus had been members of Barabbas's band of resistance fighters. One of the thieves was angry. His anger spewed out in the direction of

Jesus. He had no spirit of brokenness or sense of his own guilt. He did not see Jesus as a king to come under but only as an object of scorn and ridicule.

Actually, both of the thieves were spewing insults at Jesus in the beginning. Matthew recorded, "And the robbers who were crucified with him also reviled him in the same way" (Matt. 27:44). But then something happened. In the beginning, God had spoken creation into being in the darkness. And on this day, in the three hours of heavy darkness, God did a work of new creation by calling a spiritually dead thief to new life in the darkness of Golgotha. Though the words the thief spoke reflecting this newness of life were brief, they were revealing. Mustering enough breath to rebuke the mocking thief on the other side of Jesus, he said, "Do you not fear God, since you are under the same sentence of condemnation? And we indeed justly, for we are receiving the due reward of our deeds; but this man has done nothing wrong" (Luke 23:40–41).

This thief was dying a torturous death, and he said, "I deserve this." Very few people see their own sin that clearly. He was making no attempt to justify or defend his misspent life. Instead, he threw himself entirely and unreservedly upon Christ and asked for mercy.

> And he said, "Jesus, remember me when you come into your kingdom." And he said to him, "Truly, I say to you, today you will be with me in paradise." (Luke 23:42–43)

It's really quite amazing that this thief, agonizing in the hot sun, struggling for breath, could look at the person hanging next to him—who had been beaten and abused far worse than he had been and was clearly an object of more derision and hatred than he was—and become convinced that he was a king who had a kingdom. The thief was probably like most Jews (except for the Sadducees), in that he likely believed in a great resurrection day to come at the end of human history as we know it. In this way, he was like Martha. Remember that when Jesus said he was going to raise

Lazarus from the dead, her knowing response was, "I know that he will rise again in the resurrection on the last day" (John 11:24). Likewise, when the dying thief spoke of Jesus coming into his kingdom, he was thinking about that resurrection day that he believed was far in the future.

> And [Jesus] said to him, "Truly, I say to you, *today* you will be with me in paradise." (Luke 23:43)

This must have been surprising to the dying thief. He was not headed into some kind of soul sleep or purgatory or darkness to await a day of awakening far in the future. No, that very day he could anticipate being with Jesus in paradise, the place where all who die in Christ enjoy life in his presence as they await the resurrection. He could die in peace rather than fear, in hope rather than in despair.

In this one sentence, Jesus altered the way we understand what happens at death. Now we have something true and real to take hold of when someone we love leaves this life. We know that when the one who holds the keys to death opens that door, those we love are not plunged into an unknowing, uncaring nothingness. Rather, when Jesus opens the door of death, he's on the other side of the door! He is there to welcome all those who love him into his home, his kingdom, his presence. What a comfort this is to us when we face the death of someone we love who is in Christ, and as we face our own death.

As we consider the misconception Martha and this thief had about what happens after death, I think it helps us to see that perhaps we have the opposite misconception. Their focus was fixed on resurrection day, with little to no understanding or embrace of the intermediate state—our time in his presence as we await resurrection day. But I think most modern Christians tend toward the opposite imbalance. We tend to put our focus almost exclusively on the intermediate state, on the environment we will enter into immediately upon our death, with little to no thought of the great resurrection day to come. We tend to think about the heaven we enter into upon death as the place and the state we will remain in forever. But really, this is just a stopover. The day will come when our souls will no longer be separated from our bodies. Christ will return to this earth and call the matter of our bodies that has become dust out of our graves and will refashion it into bodies that are fit to live on a resurrected, renewed earth with him forever.

So our hope should rest firmly on both of these realities. Upon our deaths, our souls will immediately enter into the paradise of God where Christ dwells. We will be "away from the body and at home with the Lord" (2 Cor. 5:8). We will be safe in the presence of Christ until that day we return with him to this earth, when he returns in glory and power. "Our citizenship is in heaven, and from it we await a Savior, the Lord Jesus Christ, who will transform our lowly body to be like his glorious body, by the power that enables him even to subject all things to himself" (Phil. 3:20–21).

Nearly all the disciples had abandoned Jesus, assuming they had been wrong about him and his kingdom. But this dying thief believed that the man being crucified beside him was a king with a kingdom. As Jesus hung in shame, this thief believed that Jesus was the King of a glorious kingdom.

> Then Jesus, calling out with a loud voice, said, "Father, into your hands I commit my spirit!" And having said this he breathed his last. (Luke 23:46)

The one in whom the thief put all his hope was dead. But he hung on to Jesus's promise. Finally the soldiers came and broke his legs, so he would have no way to push himself up to breathe. He took his last breath there on the cross and then he awoke to take his next breath in the paradise of God. He was "away from the body and at home with the Lord" (2 Cor. 5:8).

> The dying thief rejoiced to see
> That fountain in His day;

And there have I, though vile as he,
Washed all my sins away:
Washed all my sins away,
Washed all my sins away;
And there have I, though vile as he,
Washed all my sins away.[22]

Vile as He

"And there have I, though vile as he . . ." What do you think of that? Are those just poetic words to an old song, or have you come to the point that you have seen a contamination of sin and a rebellion against God in your own soul that can only be described as vile? I think, perhaps, that if we're willing to look, we can see ourselves in nearly everyone in this scene around Jesus at his crucifixion.

Who self-righteously resisted the kingship of Jesus? Was it the religious leaders? Yes. But I must also admit #ItWasMe. I may have called Jesus "King," but so often I have not wanted to submit to him as my King. Fortunately, I can see in the story of Jesus that there is hope for me, because there was hope for some of those religious leaders. We read in the book of Acts that as Peter and the disciples proclaimed the truth about Jesus in the city of Jerusalem, something amazing happened. Acts 6:7 says, "The word of God continued to increase, and the number of the disciples multiplied greatly in Jerusalem, and a great many of the priests became obedient to the faith." Just as there was that day, there is hope for religious people today who have been blind to the reality of their own wickedness.

Who were those crowds who cried out for Jesus to be crucified? Realizing that those who demanded his crucifixion—both Jew and Gentile—represented humanity as a whole, I must admit #ItWasMe. But as the story continues, we discover that God was not finished with the crowds of people who had rejected his Son. On Pentecost, he sent his Spirit upon his people, and Peter boldly proclaimed to the crowds, "This Jesus, delivered up according to the definite plan and foreknowledge of God, you crucified and killed by the hands of lawless men. God raised him up, loosing the pangs of death, because it was not possible for him to be held by it" (Acts 2:23–24). And as Peter preached, something amazing happened.

> Now when they heard this they were cut to the heart, and said to Peter and the rest of the apostles, "Brothers, what shall we do?" And Peter said to them, "Repent and be baptized every one of you in the name of Jesus Christ for the forgiveness of your sins, and you will receive the gift of the Holy Spirit. For the promise is for you and for your children and for all who are far off, everyone whom the Lord our God calls to himself." And with many other words he bore witness and continued to exhort them, saying, "Save yourselves from this crooked generation." So those who received his word were baptized, and there were added that day about three thousand souls. (Acts 2:37–41)

Three thousand souls. A crowd of three thousand people went from being under judgment because of the blood of Jesus on their heads, to being protected from judgment by the blood of Jesus! Three thousand parents who had foolishly cried out, "His blood be on us and on our children!" believed that the promise of the gospel was for them and for their children.

> Dear dying Lamb, Thy precious blood
> Shall never lose its pow'r,
> Till all the ransomed church of God
> Be saved to sin no more:
> Be saved to sin no more,
> Be saved to sin no more;
> Till all the ransomed church of God
> Be saved, to sin no more.[23]

Who was it that was guilty and deserved to die but has been set free? On that day it was Barabbas, but though it seems too good to be true, I can say #ItWasMe! I'm a rebel. I deserve to die for my crimes of rebellion against my Creator. But an unexpected, unfathomable, undeserved exchange has taken place so that the true *bar-abbas*, the true Son of the Father—who has never done any wrong, has always obeyed, and only loved and served—took my place so that I've been set free.

We don't know what happened to Barabbas. I wonder if he made his way outside the gates of the city to hide in the crowd and catch a glimpse of the three men who were crucified that day. Did the reality that Jesus was hanging on the cross that was meant for him cause him to think differently about himself and his life? Did it make him curious about this man, Jesus, and did he ever hear that Jesus had said he came not to call the righteous but sinners? The day came when Barabbas did die. Did he die only to discover that he, in fact, had not been ultimately saved from the judgment he deserved for his rebellion and murder? Or did he close his eyes in death and discover that Jesus had not only saved him from death on the cross outside Jerusalem, but saved him from eternal death in hell?

Who confessed his sin and asked Jesus to remember him when Jesus entered into his kingdom? Yes, on that day it was the thief on the cross. But because of the mercy shown to me that brought me to repentance, I can say now, and will be celebrating into eternity, #ItWasMe! I have asked Jesus to remember me as he stands in the presence of God, and he has assured me through his word that he ever lives to intercede for me. I know that after I take my last breath in this life, I will awake to find myself with him in paradise. Jesus will remember me. He will welcome me. And one day, he will fashion for me a new body fit for living forever with him in the consummate paradise of the new heaven and new earth.

Is that your hope, your confidence? It can be, no matter who you've been or what you've done. The gospel is such good news for criminals like you and me.

For one will scarcely die for a righteous person—though per-haps for a good person one would dare even to die—but God shows his love for us in that while we were still sinners, Christ died for us. Since, therefore, we have now been justified by his blood, much more shall we be saved by him from the wrath of God. For if while we were enemies we were reconciled to God by the death of his Son, much more, now that we are recon-ciled, shall we be saved by his life. (Rom. 5:7–10)

When He comes, our glorious King,
All His ransomed home to bring,
Then anew His song we'll sing:
Hallelujah! What a Savior![24]

9

THE DISCIPLE

If I asked you to draw a line that captured the past, present, and what you hope will be the future trajectory of your life, what would that look like?

For some of us that line might trace a long season of waiting for marriage or kids or some accomplishment or attainment, and then arc upward with joy or downward in disappointment regarding those things.

For some of us that line might never be straight but demonstrate the turbulence of conflict or constant ups and downs. For others who experience depression, it might be a very flat line.

Maybe in tracing the trajectory of your life there would be a particular event—good or bad, an act of violence, an accident, some other experience—that significantly shaped it.

How do you think Joseph, the son of Jacob, would have traced the trajectory of his life? Joseph was his father's favorite son. After his dad gave him that royal coat of many colors (which indicated he would one day be head of the family), it would make sense that he expected the trajectory of his life to only go upward. Then his brothers threw him in a pit. *Down went the line.* Then they sold him as a slave. *Down.* Then he was thrown into prison. *Further down.* But then, in one day, he was lifted out of prison and set at the right hand of the king of Egypt—from the pit of prison to the pinnacle of power!

How about Job? What would the trajectory of his life look like? He was a wealthy man with the perfect family, living the good life. Then he lost everything he owned. *Down went the line.* Then he lost nearly everyone he loved. *Down.* Then he lost his health. *Down.* And in the process, he lost his reputation. *Down.* We find him sitting on a trash heap scraping his sores, wishing he could just get it all over with and die. But then God showed up and revealed himself. Job was radically restored but more than just restored. He was given double of everything he lost. Surely as Job traced the trajectory of his life, it would look like a death and then a resurrection.

How about Jesus? I think we know exactly how Jesus would trace the trajectory of his life from a couple of passages. Look at Paul's little hymn about Jesus in Philippians 2:

> Have this mind among yourselves, which is yours in Christ Jesus, who, though he was in the form of God, did not count equality with God a thing to be grasped, but emptied himself, by taking the form of a servant, being born in the likeness of men. And being found in human form, he humbled himself by becoming obedient to the point of death, even death on a cross. Therefore God has highly exalted him and bestowed on him the name that is above every name, so that at the name of Jesus every knee should bow, in heaven and on earth and under the earth, and every tongue confess that Jesus Christ is Lord, to the glory of God the Father. (Phil. 2:5–11)

Down, down, down and then *up, up, up.*

On the road to Emmaus, after his resurrection, Jesus explained to two of his followers, Cleopas and his companion, that if they had really understood the Old Testament scriptures, they would have expected that when the Christ came, his life would take exactly this trajectory—the trajectory of suffering before glory. "He said to them, 'O foolish ones, and slow of heart to believe all that the prophets have spoken! Was it not necessary that the Christ should suffer these things and enter into his glory?' And beginning with Moses and all the Prophets, he interpreted to them in all the Scriptures the things concerning himself" (Luke 24:25–27).

Evidently, while it may not have been explicit, it was clear enough in the writings of the Old Testament that those who read them should have known that the Christ would accomplish his saving work through suffering before entering his glory. Surely Jesus, in interpreting all the Scriptures concerning himself, began at the very beginning in Genesis. What was indicated about the trajectory of the life of the Messiah in Genesis 3:15? "I will put enmity between you and the woman, and between your offspring and her offspring; he shall bruise your head, and you shall bruise his heel." Suffering in having his heel bruised. Glory in dealing a deathblow to Satan.

Perhaps Jesus focused in on the lives of Joseph and Job as he talked with his two followers and pointed out the ways in which they provided living previews of his own life. Perhaps he spoke of the suffering servant of Isaiah 52 and 53 who, after being "smitten," "afflicted," "pierced," and "crushed," would be "high and lifted up and exalted" (Isa. 52:13; 53:4–5). From these passages and so many more, Cleopas and his companions should have been able to put together the suffering with the glory. But they didn't.

It is clear from the disappointment that followers of Jesus felt during his ministry when he withdrew instead of allowing the crowds to take him by force to make him king, and by their response to his death—the most ignominious death of a common criminal— that a suffering Messiah was not what the Jews had expected.

The Account of Luke

Luke, the Gospel writer, wrote a two-part version of the story of Jesus. We can think of the Gospel of Luke and the book of Acts as a two-part testimony to Jesus. Luke is an account of Jesus's ministry on earth, and Acts is an account of Jesus's ministry in heaven. It is early in Luke's Gospel that we get a hint of the suffering that will be a reality for Jesus. When Simeon took Jesus into his arms at the temple, he said that his eyes had now seen the salvation that was "for glory to your people Israel" (Luke 2:32). Glory, however, was not all Simeon saw. He saw future opposition that would cause "a sword" to pierce through Mary's soul as she would witness the suffering of her son (Luke 2:35). Luke records Jesus later saying, "A disciple is not above his teacher, but everyone when he is fully trained will be like his teacher" (Luke 6:40). Jesus got uncomfortably specific about what it was going to look like to be like him, their teacher.

> And he strictly charged and commanded them to tell this to no one, saying, "The Son of Man must suffer many things and be rejected by the elders and chief priests and scribes, and be killed, and on the third day be raised."
>
> And he said to all, "If anyone would come after me, let him deny himself and take up his cross daily and follow me. For whoever would save his life will lose it, but whoever loses his life for my sake will save it. For what does it profit a man if he gains the whole world and loses or forfeits himself? For whoever is ashamed of me and of my words, of him will the Son of Man be ashamed when he comes in his glory and the glory of the Father and of the holy angels." (Luke 9:21–26)

Jesus was going to suffer before being glorified. And he was straightforward with those who were following him that they could expect the same treatment, the same suffering.

A modern-day advertising executive might say that if Jesus was going to be successful selling this discipleship thing, he clearly needed some help. Certainly no one could ever accuse Jesus of pulling a bait-and-switch or of false advertising. His advertisement for followers basically read something like *Wanted: Disciples who are willing to leave everything familiar to follow Jesus. Carrying a cross is required. Following may result in death.*

Jesus was straightforward about what being his disciple would entail: self-denial and persecution. Somehow, I think this gets left out of many of our easy-believism invitations to faith today. What gets presented is often an invitation into a life that is going to provide an answer to all your problems; a life that will go more smoothly, not one that may become more difficult. Jesus, however, was clear about what it would cost to be his disciple. He was also clear about where being his disciple would lead. Suffering, for the disciple, would ultimately lead to glory, a glory that would outweigh the suffering.

Immediately after telling his disciples about the cross they would have to take up, we read in Luke's account that Jesus took Peter, John, and James up on a mountain and gave them a preview of this glory. Luke writes that Jesus's "face was altered, and his clothing became dazzling white" (Luke 9:29). In the transfiguration, Jesus was preparing his disciples for the suffering that lay ahead by revealing to them a glimpse of the glory they would one day share with him.

It would seem that a key purpose Luke had in writing was to prepare and strengthen Theophilus and other disciples to face opposition and persecution by highlighting parallels between the experience of Jesus in Luke and the experience of those who follow him in Acts. He wanted them to see that yes, Jesus suffered, but his suffering led to great glory. Likewise, they would suffer. He wanted to build confidence in them that after their suffering, they too would experience great glory.

We especially see this in Luke's account of the life and death of one particular disciple of Jesus named Stephen. Luke seems to have written the story of Stephen in such a way that we cannot help but draw a comparison to Jesus.

The Attributes of Stephen

We're introduced to Stephen in Acts 6, as the church in Jerusalem was just beginning to take shape. Notice in particular the words Luke used to describe the character and ministry of Stephen.

Now in these days when the disciples were increasing in number, a complaint by the Hellenists arose against the Hebrews because their widows were being neglected in the daily distribution. And the twelve summoned the full number of the disciples and said, "It is not right that we should give up preaching the word of God to serve tables. Therefore, brothers, pick out from among you seven men of good repute, full of the Spirit and of wisdom, whom we will appoint to this duty. But we will devote ourselves to prayer and to the ministry of the word." And what they said pleased the whole gathering, and they chose Stephen, a man full of faith and of the Holy Spirit, and Philip, and Prochorus, and Nicanor, and Timon, and Parmenas, and Nicolaus, a proselyte of Antioch. These they set before the apostles, and they prayed and laid their hands on them.

And the word of God continued to increase, and the number of the disciples multiplied greatly in Jerusalem, and a great many of the priests became obedient to the faith.

And Stephen, full of grace and power, was doing great wonders and signs among the people. (Acts 6:1–8)

So there was a complaint by the Hellenists, the Greek-speaking Jewish Christians that were part of the church in Jerusalem, against the Hebrew-speaking people in the church. The Hellenists were Jews who had likely lived outside of Palestine at some point, and now lived in Jerusalem where the dominant language was Hebrew. So a language barrier, and perhaps a cultural barrier, caused a breakdown that meant the Hellenist widows in the church were not getting the daily distribution of food that they needed. Something needed to be done.

In verse 2, it says "the twelve" summoned the "full number of the disciples." So the eleven apostles of Jesus plus the one who was chosen to take Judas's place, Matthias, called together all the disciples. Now we understand that when we read about "disciples" in Acts and following, we are not necessarily reading about the original twelve disciples, but rather, about all those who had joined themselves to Jesus. The twelve apostles were focused on preaching the gospel and prayer, and they realized they were going to need help to see that these kinds of practical needs were managed well. So they picked seven men of good repute, who were full of the Spirit and wisdom. These were men who would do right by these widows. One of the men chosen was Stephen, who was "a man full of faith and of the Holy Spirit."

Stephen was not just full of some general kind of faith. Rather, he was full of faith in Christ. He believed what Jesus said and what Jesus accomplished and was willing to risk everything for Jesus's sake. In verse 8, we're told that Stephen was "full of grace and power." The grace that had been extended to Stephen in Christ had changed and shaped Stephen so that he was full of grace toward others while also being courageous to confront others when needed.

The Accusation against Stephen

> Then some of those who belonged to the synagogue of the Freedmen (as it was called), and of the Cyrenians, and of the Alexandrians, and of those from Cilicia and Asia, rose up and disputed with Stephen. But they could not withstand the wisdom and the Spirit with which he was speaking. Then they secretly instigated men who said, "We have heard him speak blasphemous words against Moses and God." And they stirred up the people and the elders and the scribes, and they came upon him and seized him and brought him before the council. (Acts 6:9–12)

There was only one temple in Jerusalem, but evidently there were numerous synagogues. What was the synagogue of Freedmen? Freedmen were former slaves or the children of former slaves who had been emancipated by their owners. Many Jews who were taken captive at the time of Pompey's conquest of Judea

(AD 63) and transported to Rome, were later freed and returned to Jerusalem. Notice where those who attended this synagogue came from. The Cyrenians and Alexandrians were from North Africa, and those in Cilicia and Asia were from what we know as modern Turkey. These were Greek-speaking Jews. Perhaps Stephen was a Greek-speaking Jew since he was chosen to help serve the Greek-speaking widows. Perhaps this was the synagogue that Stephen had attended before he came to faith in Christ, and was still attending to engage with the Jews there about Jesus Christ. It would seem that when Stephen took his turn to speak at the synagogue, he likely said things like, "Now that the once-for-all perfect sacrifice has been offered, we don't need to be taking sacrifices to the temple anymore. In fact, we don't even need the temple building anymore. Jesus is the only temple we need. And while I'm at it, we really don't need to be following these cleansing rituals and ceremonial laws. Jesus has fulfilled it all. What every one of us needs to do is to leave behind all the ritual and rules and put our faith in Jesus."

As those gathered in the Freedman's synagogue listened, they became more and more angry. But they didn't know how to argue with Stephen because he supported everything he said with their own Scriptures. They "could not withstand the wisdom and the Spirit with which he was speaking" (Acts 6:10).

So what did they do? They rounded up some people who were willing to offer false testimony against Stephen before the elders and the scribes and took him to them. "And they set up false witnesses who said, 'This man never ceases to speak words against this holy place and the law, for we have heard him say that this Jesus of Nazareth will destroy this place and will change the customs that Moses delivered to us'" (Acts 6:13–14).

They were essentially saying that Stephen wouldn't quit talking about the temple and the torah—a building and a book; the place we go to find God, and the person from whom we learn how to follow God.

"And gazing at him, all who sat in the council saw that his face was like the face of an angel" (Acts 6:15). This is interesting. There's only one other person who has ever been described as having the face of an angel: Moses, when he came down from the mountain with stone tablets on which God had written his law. Just as Stephen was being accused of showing disrespect for the Law of Moses, his face began to glow in the same way Moses's face had glowed. Perhaps that should have been a sign to the council that Stephen had a better grasp on what the law of Moses meant for them at this point than they did.

Before we go on with Stephen's story, is anything about Stephen's experience sounding familiar? He was speaking with wisdom, and they couldn't stand it, yet they couldn't argue with it. They accused him of blasphemy against Moses and God. They seized him and brought him before the council of the Sanhedrin. They set up false witnesses who claimed that he was speaking against the temple and God's law. Clearly, the suffering and persecution of Stephen was taking similar shape to the suffering and persecution of Jesus.

The Argument of Stephen

"And the high priest said, 'Are these things so?'" (Acts 7:1). We hear the head of the Sanhedrin, the high priest, ask Stephen if what they were saying about him was true. *Wait a minute.* We know this guy—it's most likely Caiaphas. We might wish for him to have had some sort of breakthrough after the death and resurrection of Jesus, but evidently, he was still clinging to his power and his priesthood, devoid of grace and mercy.

Then Stephen gave a lengthy speech, and it will require a little effort on our parts to follow the argument he was making. He was responding to the two charges made against him, and that helps us to grasp two of his three primary points. Remember the charges had to do with what he said about the temple and the law of Moses. In response to the council's charges against him, Stephen sought to demonstrate: (1) God has never been confined to the temple in Jerusalem; (2) the people have never obeyed the law of Moses; and (3) the people have always killed God's prophets.

1. God has never been confined to the temple in Jerusalem.

Let's consider first the case Stephen made in response to the charge that he had spoken against the temple. Why was the temple so important to them? Remember that God's glory came down to dwell, for a time, in the Most Holy Place, the little 30 x 30-foot room in Solomon's temple. The glory of God never descended on the temple that was rebuilt after the exile or the temple that stood in Stephen's day, Herod's temple. And yet the temple was still at the heart of the Jews' identity and the source of their claim to be a people who were special to God.

Clearly, they misunderstood what the temple was always meant to be. When God gave David the blueprints for the temple, they were given so that this building would be a model of something far greater than itself. The temple was given to them to provide a tangible picture of the way God would one day deal with their sin and dwell among them. But it was always just a miniature model of a greater reality. Over time, however, they became wedded to the model and simply stopped looking for the greater reality that was still to come.

Among my grown son's old toys that are still at our house, there is a little model car. Imagine if we had given Matt this model car when he was twelve or thirteen and told him, "When you're sixteen, we're going to give you a real car. We're giving you this model to help you to anticipate that greater gift." Then imagine that when he turned sixteen, we handed him the keys to a brand-new car, just as we promised, but his response was, "No thanks. I don't want that car; I have this model car."

We would have said, "No, Matt, you don't understand. That was always just a model of something far greater that we intended to give you."

And beginning to become upset, he'd say, "Why do you want to take away my car? Don't you know how important this car is to me?"

And we would say, "But Matt, the model car simply can't get you anywhere. These are the keys to the car that can take you places."

And then he'd get outright angry: "How dare you criticize my car! This car has been in my collection for years now. How could you say something as evil as you are saying about my car?"

That sounds crazy, right?

But this was the situation with the people and the temple. The temple was always merely a model of something greater that God intended to give to his people in the person of Jesus. How did Stephen make his point? He worked his way through a theological geography lesson, tracing Israel's history, including her most important people, and demonstrating that the glory of God had never been confined to a temple in Jerusalem. His words are recorded for us in Acts 7:

v. 2: The glory of God appeared to Abraham *in Mesopotamia*.

v. 9: God was with Joseph *in Egypt*.

vv. 30—33: The Angel of the Lord appeared to Moses *in the wilderness* in the form of a burning bush so that God called that place "holy ground."

v. 38: God spoke to Moses *at Mount Sinai*.

v. 48: Stephen articulated his conclusion. Yes, Solomon built a house for God. "Yet the Most High *does not dwell in houses made by hands*."

vv. 49–50: Then Stephen quoted God speaking through the prophet Isaiah to back up his conclusion:

"Heaven is my throne,
  and the earth is my footstool.
What kind of house will you build for me, says the Lord,
  or what is the place of my rest?
Did not my hand make all these things?"

Stephen's clear response to the council's first accusation regarding his supposed disregard for the temple was that God had never been confined to the temple in Jerusalem. So why were they unwilling to accept that God's presence had shifted away from the temple in Jerusalem at this point?

The members of this council had turned the temple into an idol—as if it were the only location for God's presence, to be maintained at all costs. Through his arguments, Stephen had relativized the temple. Did you catch that Stephen was hinting that they'd made the temple into an idol? Notice verse 41. When the people of Israel made the golden calf (an idol), they "were rejoicing in the works of their hands." Then in verse 48, Stephen quoted Isaiah saying that God does not live in "houses made by hands"; rather, according to verse 50, God's hands have made his holy habitation.

Throughout the Old Testament, idols were always mocked as being made by human hands and yet worshiped. Stephen was pointing out that the temple was made by human hands. While God did condescend to inhabit the Most Holy Place of the temple at times in Israel's history, God had never been confined to the temple in Jerusalem. The temple in Jerusalem was always merely a model of a greater temple, the true temple, the person of Jesus Christ. The people needed to release their grip on the model, which had become an idol, and take hold of the greater temple, the person of Jesus.

This was an important message for the people of Stephen's day. But there's an important lesson in it for us as well. It's not about where we go to meet with God; rather, it's about the God who comes to meet with us. It's about the God who has promised again and again, "I will be with you." Stephen was telling them then, and is telling us now, that God has come down to meet with us through Immanuel, God with us, Jesus.

2. The people have never obeyed the Law of Moses.

The second accusation the council made against Stephen was that he had spoken against the law, that he wanted to change the customs that Moses had delivered to them. Of course, they said this as if they had actually honored and obeyed the law that Moses had given to them. So the second thing Stephen sought to demonstrate through his history lesson was that those who were accusing him of speaking against Moses came from a long line of people who had refused to obey the law of Moses. Stephen pointed out two choice examples of their rejection of the law of Moses:

> v. 41: While the Israelites were still in the wilderness, they made a golden calf and offered sacrifices to it.
>
> v. 43: Once the Israelites were in the promised land, they began worshiping heavenly bodies such as the Canaanite sun god, Moloch.
>
> vv. 51–53: Then Stephen concluded saying that the Jews were still stiff-necked, uncircumcised in heart, and resistant to the Holy Spirit, just as their ancestors were: "You . . . received the law as delivered by angels and did not keep it."

They had charged him with wanting to change the law given by Moses, but they had never obeyed God's law given to Moses themselves.

3. The people have always killed God's prophets.

The third thing Stephen's speech demonstrated was that their persecution of him was nothing new. Throughout Israel's history, the people had always responded with violence against those who spoke God's word to them.

> v. 9: Joseph's brothers, the patriarchs, tried to kill Joseph but then sold him into slavery because they were so angry with him over telling them about the word of God that came to him in his dream, which suggested they would one day bow down to him.
>
> v. 27: The Israelites in bondage in Egypt said to Moses, who was to be their deliverer, "Who made you a ruler and a judge over us?"
>
> v. 35: The Israelites resented, and ultimately rejected, Moses.

v. 37: Moses had said that there was going to be another prophet like him, yet greater than him, who they should listen to. But when that greater prophet came, they didn't listen to him; they killed him. Stephen was saying that in rejecting and killing Jesus, it was they (rather than he) who were guilty of being "against Moses." They rejected the one to whom Moses and the law pointed.

vv. 38–39 Moses was given the "living oracles" but, Stephen says, "our fathers refused to obey [Moses] but thrust him aside and, in their hearts, turned to Egypt."

v. 52: The generations that followed persecuted and killed many of the prophets "who announced beforehand the coming of the Righteous One, whom you have now betrayed and murdered."

They rejected Joseph when he prophesied about the future. They rejected Moses when he spoke for God to them. They rejected and killed many of the prophets who spoke to them about the greater prophet to come. And then they killed the ultimate prophet, Jesus. They had always rejected and killed God's prophets. Surely Stephen didn't think they would treat him any differently.

As we think about the charges made against Stephen and the points he made in response, we realize he was sounding a lot like Jesus. Jesus was clear that the temple in Jerusalem had always been most profoundly about him. Jesus was clear that he had come not to abolish but to fulfill the law of Moses. Jesus indicted the Jewish leaders for killing the prophets. So not only was Stephen's character and ministry much like Jesus's, and not only was the treatment he received much like the treatment Jesus had received, even Stephen's responses to the accusations of the Jewish leaders sounded very much like Jesus's. And, just as the words of Jesus so enraged those whose hearts were so hard that they wanted to kill Jesus, so Stephen's words made these religious leaders so enraged, they wanted to kill Stephen.

The Advocate for Stephen

> Now when they heard these things they were enraged, and
> they ground their teeth at him. But he, full of the Holy Spirit,
> gazed into heaven and saw the glory of God, and Jesus standing
> at the right hand of God. And he said, "Behold, I see the heav-
> ens opened, and the Son of Man standing at the right hand of
> God." (Acts 7:54–56)

Stephen's speech had explored where the glory of God had mani-
fested itself throughout the history of God's people—in Mesopotamia, in the wilderness, in Egypt—and on that day before the council
Stephen saw the glory of God with his own eyes. He'd just quoted
Psalm 11 and Isaiah 66 about God's throne in heaven, and now heaven
opened and he could see God's throne! He could see his advocate
standing there, pleading his case, preparing to welcome him in.

The Sanhedrin had encouraged false witnesses to stand and
give their testimony against both Jesus and Stephen in their court.
But now Stephen saw into the heavenly courtroom. And Jesus,
who is faithful and true, was standing there giving his testimony
concerning Stephen. He was doing as he promised when he said,
"Whoever acknowledges me before men, the Son of Man will also
acknowledge him before the angels of God" (Luke 12:8).

Really, this was the culmination of Stephen's tracing of the
location of the glory of God. It was not in the temple in Jerusalem.
Jesus was in the heavenly throne room, and he was standing to
welcome Stephen into the place of God's glorious presence.

As we see how God opened up the heavens for this disciple, it
should give us courage to face whatever suffering this life throws
at us. Confidence in the glory of the future enables us to endure
the suffering of the present. Knowing that we have an Advocate
standing up for us in heaven emboldens us to face whatever is
said against us here.

> But they cried out with a loud voice and stopped their ears and
> rushed together at him. Then they cast him out of the city and

stoned him. And the witnesses laid down their garments at the feet of a young man named Saul. And as they were stoning Stephen, he called out, "Lord Jesus, receive my spirit." And falling to his knees he cried out with a loud voice, "Lord, do not hold this sin against them." And when he had said this, he fell asleep. (Acts 7:57–60)

In contrast to the angry rage that came down on him, Stephen had two dying prayers on his lips that marked him out as a disciple of Jesus. Oh, that we would die with as much faith and grace as Stephen. We likely won't face death by stoning, but no matter what brings about our deaths, we do want to die distinctly as disciples of Christ.

"Lord Jesus, receive my spirit." Stephen, the man who was described as "full of faith," showed us how a person who is full of faith dies—confident in what Jesus has promised, that to be absent from the body is to be present with the Lord. He was not fearfully, desperately clutching onto life here. He hadn't gathered everyone around to pray for the miracle of a longer life. He peacefully entered into the joy of his Master. What a way to die: full of faith. He lived like his Master, suffered like his Master, and now he died like his Master, who had said from the cross, "Father, into your hands I commit my spirit!" (Luke 23:46).

And not only did Stephen die as a disciple who was full of faith, he died as a disciple who was full of grace, saying, "Lord, do not hold this sin against them." Full of grace for those who were hurling stones at him. He was dying like his Master, who said as he died, "Father, forgive them, for they know not what they do" (Luke 23:34). Jesus was full of grace for those who nailed him to the cross, mocked him, spit on him, and slapped him.

It is interesting that Luke does not write that Stephen died. He writes that he "fell asleep." He's communicating something about the reality of death for a disciple of Jesus. For the person who has suffered with Jesus and died anticipating the glory of Jesus, death is not really death. It is merely falling asleep, awaiting the resurrection morning call of the Master.

Stephen's death must have looked to the early church like such a waste, such a tragedy, such a miscarriage of justice. But they would come to see that what Jesus had said was really true. Jesus said, "Truly, truly, I say to you, unless a grain of wheat falls into the earth and dies, it remains alone; but if it dies, it bears much fruit." This was true not only in the death of Jesus, but also in the death of Stephen, his disciple.

> And there arose on that day a great persecution against the church in Jerusalem, and they were all scattered throughout the regions of Judea and Samaria, except the apostles. (Acts 8:1)

As persecution increased in Jerusalem, disciples were dispersed outside of Jerusalem, throughout Judea and Samaria, and eventually to the ends of the earth. The seed of the gospel was spread throughout the world. The glory of God spread as more and more people from every tribe, tongue, and nation embraced Christ and were made into living stones, being built together into a dwelling place for God, the worldwide church. If we were to continue reading in Acts 8, we'd see Samaritans who were barred from entering the temple in Jerusalem, invited into the temple that is the person of Jesus Christ. We'd see eunuchs who were barred from entering the temple in Jerusalem, invited into the temple that is the person of Jesus Christ.

And as Theolophilus—the original recipient of Luke's orderly account—as well as the other early Christians who lived in the reality of opposition read what Luke wrote about the death of Stephen, the truth would sink in that glory on the other side of suffering was not merely theoretical, sentimental, or mystical—it was real. By reading Luke's parallel accounts of the suffering before glory of Jesus and Stephen, Theophilus and readers of Acts would grow in their confidence that they too would enter into glory when the suffering of this life came to an end.

Even now, Luke's account has the power to fill disciples like you and me with faith to face whatever suffering comes in this life as we anticipate the glory to follow.

I don't know what the trajectory of your life is going to look like from here. I do know that as you live your life in a world under a curse, you will experience the suffering of this life that is common to everyone. Some of you are experiencing that right now—the pain of childbearing as you, a sinner, raise a sinner in a sin-cursed world. Some of you are experiencing the suffering of difficulty and conflict in your marriage, and some are suffering the disappointment that you are not married. Some of you have lives marked by the frustration and lack of fulfillment of life in this world under a curse. Some of you are living in bodies that are a constant reminder that these bodies have been impacted by the curse of sin.

And some of you know what it is to suffer uniquely for your allegiance to Christ, your service to Christ, your declaration of Christ. We've had a lot of years of freedom from persecution living here in the West, but that hasn't been the case in most parts of the world. Most of us know very little of real suffering for our connection to Christ. But the tide may be turning. There may be some among us who begin losing our jobs because we are unwilling to go with the flow of corruption or contribution to ungodly causes. There may be some here who begin to feel the squeeze as what we have deemed to be raising our children in the nurture and admonition of the Lord gets labeled as "unfit parenting." There may be some here who are no longer welcome around the table of extended family, on the soccer sidelines, on the parents' council, or on the city council because of an unwillingness to neither tolerate nor celebrate the sin of others. You may be labeled intolerant, even immoral, for your unwavering commitment to holiness.

The writer of Hebrews said it was "for the joy that was set before him [that Christ] endured the cross" (Heb. 12:2). The joy that was set before Jesus that enabled him to endure the cross was the glory of resurrection! It was the glory of a future seated at the right hand of the throne of God. The glory of the future enabled Jesus to endure the suffering in the present as he faced the cross. Likewise, the glory of a future in the presence of Christ enabled Stephen to endure the suffering in his present as he faced a cruel mob throwing stones.

I don't know what that line representing the trajectory of your life is going to look like for you on this earth. But I am sure of one thing: anticipation of future glory has the power to instill patient endurance of suffering in the present.

If you are in Christ, the day is coming when the trajectory of your life is going to take a dramatic turn, a dramatic turn upward. The day that some people may think is the worst day of your life will not prove to be so. Instead it will be the very best day of your life. It will be the day when the trajectory of your life pivots away from the suffering of this life toward the glory of Jesus. One day, my friends, your suffering will give way to great glory—joyful glory, peaceful glory, eternal glory!

The glory of God is not bound up in a cube at the center of a room in a temple in Jerusalem. We're not waiting for that temple to be rebuilt. You don't have to make a pilgrimage there or anywhere else to experience the presence of God. As you take hold of Jesus by faith, his glorious presence comes now to rest on you, abide in you, and work through you. You can begin now to anticipate the day when you will enter into the fullness of his glory to enjoy him forever. If you are in Christ, that is where the trajectory of your life is headed.

> O for a thousand tongues to sing
> My great Redeemer's praise,
> The glories of my God and King,
> The triumphs of His grace.
>
> Jesus! the name that charms our fears,
> That bids our sorrows cease,

'Tis music in the sinner's ears,
'Tis life and health and peace.

To God all glory, praise, and love
Be now and ever given
By saints below and saints above,
The church in earth and heaven.[25]

10

THE WORST

Who is the last person in the world that you think will ever become a Christian?

Is it someone we hear about on the news? Someone like Abubakar Shekau, the leader of the Nigerian militant group Boko Haram, which kidnapped over two hundred schoolgirls in 2014 and forced many of them to marry Boko Haram soldiers? Is it Kim Jong-un, the supreme leader of North Korea, the world's most oppressive dictatorship, who has starved his own people while presenting to the world that they are healthy and happy—and whose 200,000 political prisoners include 70,000 Christians?

Or is it someone like Woody Allen, whose trademark black humor reflects strong atheist convictions, emphasizing the futility of human existence? Or atheist author Sam Harris who has written that his aim is "to demolish the intellectual and moral pretensions of Christianity in its most committed forms"?

More likely, the last person in the world you think will ever become a Christian is someone who is closer to you than any of these people. Perhaps it's your mom or dad, aunt or uncle. Someone who has spent a lifetime, perhaps, being a very good person but who sees no need for dependence on Christ. Perhaps it is a sibling who has left behind the faith you both grew up with. Maybe it is someone you know who experienced sexual abuse at the hands of someone who claimed to be a Christian, or someone you know who simply cannot accept a God who would disapprove of a homosexual relationship.

Or perhaps the last person you think will ever become a Christian is you. Maybe you have lingering doubts about the truth claims of the Bible or the exclusivity of Christ so that you cannot ever imagine giving your wholehearted allegiance to Christ. Maybe it is not so much what you think of the God of the Bible, but what you know about yourself, that has created what seems to be an insurmountable distance between you and saving faith. Perhaps there is a sin in your past that, deep down, you think exempts you from being a recipient of grace and mercy. Maybe it was an abortion or an affair. Perhaps you still feel dirty from abuse you received. Or perhaps you carry the secret of being an abuser. Whatever it may be, you see yourself as unforgivable, and therefore the idea of becoming a Christian seems an exercise in hypocrisy.

If you think that someone in your world is too far away from Christ to ever take hold of him, or if you think that your own record of wrong is too great to be forgiven by him, then the story we're looking at in this final chapter is especially for you. If the Christians who lived in those first few years after the life, death, resurrection, and ascension of Jesus had been asked, "Who is the last person you think will ever become a Christian?" certainly many would have answered, "Saul of Tarsus."

Saul, the Hebrew of Hebrews

Saul of Tarsus was perhaps the most notorious opponent of Jesus and his cause. A callous, self-righteous, bigoted murderer, Saul's hands were covered in the blood of Christians.

Saul was one of the many Jews in his day who lived away from the land of Palestine. He grew up in the busy streets and crowded bazaars of the city of Tarsus, a Greek city devoted to learning. Saul's family was one of many families in Tarsus who were weavers of goats' hair, which they made into dark, coarse cloth known as "Cilician cloth." This cloth was suitable for making into tents. With all the Roman soldiers living in tents around the Roman Empire, there was likely plenty of demand for this product.

Clearly Saul's family was committed to the faith of their ancestors. He was, as he would write later, "a Hebrew of Hebrews," meaning that on both his mother's and his father's side, his Jewish genealogy was pure. Evidently the household he grew up in took the rabbinic laws very seriously, as Saul was circumcised on the eighth day. On that day, he was given a double name—Saul, the name of his ancestor, the first king of Israel, for the Jewish part of his life; and Paul, for his life of trade in a Greek city. Saul wrote that he was "blameless," which meant that there was no precept in the moral or ceremonial law that he consciously disregarded. This means that he would never have gone into the home of his Gentile neighbors in Tarsus or eaten a meal that they had prepared. He would have fasted twice a week and tithed everything he possessed. He and his family would have scrupulously observed the Sabbath and the Jewish feasts and festivals.

By the time he was five years old, Saul was probably already learning to read the books of the Old Testament. At six, he would have begun to be schooled by a rabbi so that he would become immersed in the law. Then, between the ages of thirteen and sixteen, we know that Saul was sent to Jerusalem to study under the respected teacher of the law, Gamaliel. Every day there would have been spent in careful study of the words of the law along with interpretations of the law taught by various rabbis.

A passion for God's law as the party of the Pharisees understood and applied it was instilled in Saul under Gamaliel. When Saul's training was complete, he likely returned to Tarsus to take up the family business as he continued his study to become a rabbi himself. It seems Saul was not in Jerusalem during the years when Jesus occasionally visited the temple. But after the resurrection and ascension of Jesus, as Jewish people in and around Jerusalem began to espouse belief in Jesus as the Messiah, Saul evidently returned to Jerusalem. There in the temple, he began to encounter followers of "the Way"—Jews who were still observing Jewish rights and feasts but were arguing that Jesus of Nazareth was the Messiah and had risen from the dead and ascended into heaven. To Saul and so many of his fellow Pharisees, the idea of a humiliated, suffering, dying Messiah was pure blasphemy. And while they did believe in a great resurrection to come, they decidedly did not believe that Jesus had been resurrected from the dead.

The religious leaders in Jerusalem evidently took note of Saul's zeal for squashing what he saw as a perversion of the Jewish faith. They put him in charge of the no-holds-barred offensive against any and all people who had turned away from righteousness through law keeping (as taught by the rabbis) and toward righteousness through faith in the risen Jesus. Paul later explained,

> I myself was convinced that I ought to do many things in opposing the name of Jesus of Nazareth. And I did so in Jerusalem. I not only locked up many of the saints in prison after receiving authority from the chief priests, but when they were put to death I cast my vote against them. (Acts 26:9–10)

Saul was convinced. He was convinced that this man, Jesus of Nazareth, was not the Messiah, and that he certainly was not resurrected from the dead. Saul was so zealous to protect the law of God from what he saw as a corruption and defiance of that law that his zeal became murderous. The Bible offers its first glimpse of Saul standing and watching as the men of Jerusalem hurled huge stones at Stephen that broke his bones, bloodied his body, and eventually took his life. We read in Acts 8:1 that "Saul approved of his execution." But perhaps that is an understatement. Evidently, it whetted Saul's appetite for more. We read that as "Saul was ravaging the church, and entering house after house, he dragged off men and women and committed them to prison" (v. 3).

These images may still be stuck on the Sunday school felt board in our minds, lacking the reality of what this situation was like in real life. Perhaps you've seen a movie in which Nazi soldiers break into a home, drag away young and old alike, and load them onto a train to be herded into a prison camp or gas chamber. Saul seems to fit right in with the coldest, cruelest characters we've ever seen in movies as we read that Saul, "breathing threats and murder against the disciples of the Lord, went to the high priest and asked him for letters to the synagogues at Damascus, so that if he found any belonging to the Way, men or women, he might bring them bound to Jerusalem" (Acts 9:1–2).

Hatred for Jesus and those who were connected to him became such a part of Saul that he ate and slept and breathed out that hatred. It was not enough for him to put the Christians in Jerusalem and its surrounding cities in prison. He was out to chase down and snuff out any and all Jews who had fled to foreign cities. So he set his sights on the nearest large city outside the borders of Palestine and packed his bags. He put together a group of men who would not hesitate to drag old men out of their beds and mothers away from their children. He was going to tie them up and march them back in chains to Jerusalem, and if any of them should not survive the trip, it was of no concern to him. He was a hunter of human beings, and he was good at it.

Saul was carrying out the religious equivalent of ethnic cleansing. And he had no moral quandary about it. He was convinced that Jesus was dead and that what he was doing was right. We read in John 16 that Jesus had said to his disciples in the upper room, "They will put you out of the synagogues. Indeed, the hour is coming when whoever kills you will think he is offering service to God" (John 16:2). And of course, that was exactly how Saul thought of himself and his murderous plans. He saw himself as carrying out the command of Leviticus 24:16, which says, "Whoever blas-phemes the name of the LORD shall surely be put to death." His persecution of the church was rooted in his understanding and practice of the law. "I myself was convinced that I ought to do many things in opposing the name of Jesus of Nazareth," Saul would later explain to King Agrippa (Acts 26:9). He was sincere in his beliefs—sincerely, murderously wrong.

So Saul set out for Damascus. He had the letter in his pocket from the high priest in Jerusalem that he planned to present to the leaders of the synagogue in Damascus. He would compel them to name the names of those who had dared to speak about Jesus in the synagogue or who were gathering on the first day of the week because they claimed Jesus was raised on the first day of the week. Perhaps Saul was composing a speech in his mind to whip the synagogue-goers into a hateful frenzy toward their Jesus-following neighbors. Perhaps he was imagining the praise he would receive from the members of the Sanhedrin when he came home with a procession of human beings in chains.

But then, something happened. "Now as he went on his way, he approached Damascus, and suddenly a light from heaven shone around him (Acts 9:3). It was the middle of the day and the sun was in the sky, but this was not the sun; it was "a light from heaven, brighter than the sun" (Acts 26:13). This light from heaven was, in fact, the radiant glory of the face of the risen Jesus shining down so brightly on Saul that he was blinded by it. The human features of Jesus were looking down on Saul through the open doorway of heaven. The blinding light was crippling, but the question asked by the voice coming from the light was confusing.

> And falling to the ground, he heard a voice saying to him, "Saul, Saul, why are you persecuting me?" And he said, "Who are you, Lord?" And he said, "I am Jesus, whom you are perse-cuting." (Acts 9:4–5)

Surely Saul would have preferred any other answer to his question than the one he received. The Jesus that he thought was dead was clearly not dead. And not only was he not dead, he was the living Lord of the universe. He took Saul's assault on those who had put their hope in him very personally. There, with his face to the ground, it began to dawn on Saul that Jesus was so united to those who loved and believed in Christ that every cruel thing Saul had done to any one of them, he had done to Jesus. Saul's murderous hatred breathed onto followers of "the Way" was actually hatred toward the one who gave him breath.

> The men who were traveling with him stood speechless, hearing the voice but seeing no one. Saul rose from the ground, and although his eyes were opened, he saw nothing. So they led him by the hand and brought him into Damascus. And for three days he was without sight, and neither ate nor drank. (Acts 9:6–9)

What must have gone through Saul's mind as he sat in the dark for those three days? F. B Meyer writes about this time: "It is an awful discovery when a great light from heaven shows a man that what he has regarded his solemn duty has been one long sin against the dearest purposes of God."[26] There in the darkness, a light was coming on in the interior of Saul's soul.

> Now there was a disciple at Damascus named Ananias. The Lord said to him in a vision, "Ananias." And he said, "Here I am, Lord." And the Lord said to him, "Rise and go to the street called Straight, and at the house of Judas look for a man of Tarsus named Saul, for behold, he is praying, and he has seen in a vision a man named Ananias come in and lay his hands on him so that he might regain his sight." But Ananias answered, "Lord, I have heard from many about this man, how much evil he has done to your saints at Jerusalem. And here he has authority from the chief priests to bind all who call on your name." (Acts 9:10–14)

Word had made it all the way to Damascus—not just about the harm that had been done by Saul to believers in Jerusalem, but about his plan to put the believers in Damascus in chains and drag them back to Jerusalem to be imprisoned or executed. Imagine the fear in the homes of believers in Damascus. Surely they were praying for protection from Saul, praying that he would not lay hands on them to drag them away. And then Ananias was told in a divine vision that he was to go and lay hands on Saul, not to harm him but to heal him.

> But the Lord said to him, "Go, for he is a chosen instrument of mine to carry my name before the Gentiles and kings and the children of Israel. For I will show him how much he must suffer for the sake of my name." (Acts 9:15–16)

This must have been shocking to Ananias. Out of all the people in the world that God could choose to use to make the gospel of Jesus Christ known—not just to Jews, but to Gentiles, people who had never known Yahweh—Saul was the one God had chosen. Perhaps Ananias knew and loved Stephen or other Jews who had been put to death by Saul. That would have made this news especially hard to swallow. I think if I were Ananias, I would have dragged my feet in carrying out this mission. But not Ananias.

> So Ananias departed and entered the house. And laying his hands on him he said, "Brother Saul, the Lord Jesus who appeared to you on the road by which you came has sent me so that you may regain your sight and be filled with the Holy Spirit." And immediately something like scales fell from his eyes, and he regained his sight. (Acts 9:17–18)

Three days of blindness had enabled Saul to see that all his life he had been living in spiritual darkness. Everything he had lived for had been all wrong. Saul was no longer filled with murderous rage but was now filled with the Holy Spirit.

"Then he rose and was baptized; and taking food, he was strengthened. For some days he was with the disciples at Damascus" (Acts 9:18–19). The one who had been breathing threats against them became the brother beside them. The blasphemer had become a baptized believer. "And immediately he proclaimed Jesus in the synagogues, saying, 'He is the Son of God'" (Acts 9:20). The religious predator had become a gospel preacher!

"And all who heard him were amazed and said, 'Is not this the man who made havoc in Jerusalem of those who called upon this name? And has he not come here for this purpose, to bring them bound before the chief priests?'" (Acts 9:21). The hunter had been captured by grace.

Something supernatural happened to Saul on that road and in the house of Judas on the street called Straight. There was Saul, the most unlikely person in his day to ever become a Christian, and God supernaturally intervened. His conversion was not the climax of a long process of God convicting him of sin or someone else convincing him with a sound argument. Jesus supernaturally revealed himself to Saul in such a way that it overcame Saul's ignorance about who Jesus was, his opposition to belief in Jesus, and his pride in his own record of religious observance. The risen, glorified Jesus summoned Saul, not only to come to him but to serve him, overcoming all Saul's resistance. Saul wrote later that God, who "had set me apart before I was born, and who called me by his grace, was pleased to reveal his Son to me, in order that I might preach him among the Gentiles" (Gal. 1:15–16). If Saul was set apart for this before he was born, then we realize that God had been sovereign over every day of his life. God had been working out his plan in Saul's life. Being raised in a Gentile city prepared him to take the gospel to Gentiles. Being schooled in the Scriptures prepared him to preach from the Scriptures. Having been given two names at birth, one for his Jewish life and one for his life in the marketplace, equipped him to become Paul, the apostle to the Gentiles. God had been working out his plan for Saul—in his timing—over the course of a life mired in sin.

In the same way, if the person you know who has so far rejected Christ is ever going to be joined to Christ, something supernatural must happen. And it will only happen in God's timing not yours. In God's timing, and in his way, a revelation of who Jesus is must overcome that person's ignorant unbelief, passionate opposition, and prideful resistance to Jesus.

A Revelation of Who Jesus Is

Sometimes we think that it is information that our unbelieving family members or friends need most—that if they will just read this book or listen to this talk, then they will see and understand and believe. But here was Saul; he had spent more hours than you or me studying the Scriptures, yet he remained blind to the truth. Something supernatural had to happen for him to be transformed from ignorant to illumined. This same supernatural revelation is what is needed for the person you care about to finally see and believe in Jesus. No one's eyes are opened to who Jesus is without this supernatural revelation. When Peter came to the place that he was able to say to Jesus, "You are the Christ, the Son of the living God," we read that Jesus answered him by saying, "Flesh and blood has not revealed this to you, but my Father who is in heaven" (Matt. 16:16–17).

Is it perhaps passion for something other than Christ that causes you to think it impossible that your loved one will ever come to Christ? Do you think it is impossible that someone who makes such passionate arguments against Christianity could ever become a passionate lover of Christ? Take stock of Saul's anti-Christ passion and pray that the passionate opposition to Christ you see in the person you care about will be transformed by a supernatural work of God into passionate love for Christ and a passion to live for Christ.

Imagine the humility required for Saul to admit that he had been so very wrong about Jesus—publicly, devastatingly wrong. Imagine the regret he must have felt over the pain and anguish his egregious error and cruelty brought into the lives of those who were now his brothers and sisters in Christ. Only the Spirit of Christ at work in a prideful, resistant person can enable her to humble herself to face being so very wrong about Jesus. The humility required to admit that you have been wrong *about* Jesus must be supernaturally provided *by* Jesus.

Should you keep on testifying about Christ to that person in your life you think is dead set against faith in Christ? *Yes.* Should you invite that person who has no interest in Christ to sit with you under the preaching of God's word or give them a book that clearly presents the gospel? *Yes.* Should you keep on reasoning with that person who always seems to have yet another hard-to-answer argument against faith in Christ? *Yes.* But the most important thing you can do in regard to the last person you would ever expect to come to Christ is to pray that God will do a supernatural work in that person's life that only God can do. No one is ever saved without having their blindness regarding Jesus healed and their resistance to Jesus removed in a supernatural work of God. Everyone who becomes united to Christ can share the same testimony with Saul, which is, "The God who said, 'Let light shine out of darkness,' has shone in [my] heart to give the light of the knowledge of the glory of God in the face of Christ" (2 Cor. 4:6).

As we gaze into what was involved in Saul's change from an enemy of Christ into a servant of Christ, we realize that in addition to experiencing a revelation of who Jesus is, a person must also reevaluate what is truly worthwhile, coming to a new estimation of the supreme worth of Jesus.

A Reevaluation of What Jesus Is Worth

Looking back on his own experience of this period of reevaluation of what was worthwhile, Paul wrote to the believers in Philippi that he was

> circumcised on the eighth day, of the people of Israel, of the tribe of Benjamin, a Hebrew of Hebrews; as to the law,

a Pharisee; as to zeal, a persecutor of the church; as to righteousness under the law, blameless. But whatever gain I had,
I counted as loss for the sake of Christ. Indeed, I count everything as loss because of the surpassing worth of knowing
Christ Jesus my Lord." (Phil. 3:5–10)

Saul came to see that Jesus was worth more than his family
identity, more than his record of religious adherence, more than
all his presumed goodness, more than the approval of the Sanhedrin. He lost everything that had given him a sense of worth and
identity, except now he had Jesus.

We are so far removed from the first century, we have a hard
time imagining what it would have meant for someone who
was a Hebrew of Hebrews, born into the tribe of Benjamin, to
come to see all that family heritage as of no value to him. In
fact, it had actually been a hindrance to having true meaning
in Saul's life. We can only begin to imagine the tension of being
the person who had been put in charge of persecuting and im-
prisoning Jewish believers in Christ, but who now stood before
the Sanhedrin contending for Christ. We can barely imagine
what it meant for someone who had spent every day of his life
washing, fasting, and avoiding all the unclean things, changing
enough to write across all those practices: "nothing," "rubbish,"
"worthless."

But maybe we can begin to imagine what it would cost for our
Muslim neighbor to be disowned by her family, or our Jewish co-
worker to be disinherited from his family and unwelcome to Shab-
bat. Maybe we can imagine what it would be like for the college
professor who has led in the battle for LGBTQ acceptance to espouse an allegiance to Christ and a call to sexual purity.[27] If you're
someone who grew up in church, and you know all the words to
the Christian songs and all the Christian jargon, and you have sat
through a thousand sermons, and then one day realize that none
of that has been of any benefit to you, then perhaps you have a

sense of what it costs to come to truly treasure Christ more than anything else in this world.

To become a Christian is not merely to agree with a set of facts about Christ or to see that he is, in fact, the Christ. It is to experience a radical reordering of what is valuable so that nothing is more valuable in the universe and in your life than Christ. Being identified with him is more valuable than having an impressive reputation. Living under his authority is more valuable than doing as you please. Becoming more like him is more important than expressing yourself. Having him reorder your loves is more desirable than getting what you've always wanted.

And the reality is that no one comes to this radical shift without having their eyes supernaturally opened to the supreme worth of Jesus. Have your eyes been opened to the beauty and sufficiency and riches in Christ Jesus so that you have been able to write across the things this world values apart from Christ: "nothing," "rubbish," "worthless"?

In addition to a revelation of who Jesus is and a reevaluation of what Jesus is worth, there is another thing we see in the salvation of Saul, the most unlikely convert, that must also become a reality in the life of anyone whose life is truly changed by Christ. There must be an openness to receiving the grace and mercy that only comes through Christ.

A Reception of What Jesus Gives

When Saul was blinded by the glory of Jesus on the road to Damascus, there was something he could finally see that he had not seen clearly before. He saw himself in the light of the radiant holiness of Jesus, and for the first time he saw himself as a sinner. In fact, because Saul then knew the interior of his heart, the corruption of his motives, the selfishness of his own thoughts and attitudes far better than anyone else, he later wrote, "The saying is trustworthy and deserving of full acceptance, that Christ Jesus came into the world to save sinners, of whom I am the foremost" (1 Tim. 1:15).

Different Bible translations use different terms here—"the worst" of sinners (NIV), "chief" of sinners (KJV), "foremost" sinner. A few verses before this, Paul gave a rundown of sins and sinners—"those who strike their fathers and mothers, . . . murderers, the sexually immoral, men who practice homosexuality, enslavers, liars, perjurers, and whatever else is contrary to sound doctrine" (1 Tim. 1:9–10). But he was quick to make sure Timothy understood that when Paul talked about sinners, he was not pointing his finger at others. It was pointed squarely at himself. Yet he was not merely pointing to himself as "Exhibit A in Notorious Sinners"; he was pointing to himself as the prime example of a sinner saved by grace. He continued, "But I received mercy for this reason, that in me, as the foremost, Jesus Christ might display his perfect patience as an example to those who were to believe in him for eternal life" (1 Tim. 1:16). Paul pointed to himself in order to give hope to any and all who might be tempted to think that they are somehow too far gone, that they've done something too terrible, that they are somehow beyond being candidates for mercy.

You see, before Paul was converted, he was not only blind to who Jesus was, he was also blind to who and what he, Paul, really was. Only the person who has had the light of Christ shine into her life—a light intended to generate not shame but clarity about her real condition—is in a position to receive mercy. The light of the holiness of Jesus reveals the sin-sickness, the spiritual darkness, the truth about how deep our sin goes and how pervasive its reach is.

We often think of the worst sinners as being people who do the things on our list of terrible, immoral sins. But if the greatest good in the universe is the triune God, then the greatest evil in the universe is to defy, to ignore, to refuse the good gifts of that God.

The worst of sinners needs the greatest of Saviors, and that's what we have. That's who we have in Jesus Christ. "While we were still sinners, Christ died for us" (Rom. 5:8). This Savior is our Savior. This grace is our grace. Seeing into the conversion and transformation of Saul should fill every one of us with hope. When we look at Saul, we can't help but recognize that there is no sinner, no scoundrel, no blasphemer, no murderer, no person who is beyond the reach of the grace and mercy made available in Jesus Christ.

Throughout this book, we've been talking about saints and scoundrels. And perhaps you find it a stretch to call yourself a saint even though you would call yourself a Christian. My friend, a saint is not someone who is free of sin; a saint is someone who is no longer under condemnation for sin or controlled by sin. A saint is someone who has been humbled by the reality of her sinful impulses, her sin-infected motives, and her sin-stained record. But instead of being constantly crushed by this reality, she finds herself constantly grateful for a far greater reality—the reality of the grace and mercy extended to her in the person and work of Jesus Christ. This grace keeps drawing her to turn toward Christ in sorrow over her sin. She keeps finding that this grace is giving her power to forsake sin.

This grace is freely available to the last person you expect to become a Christian, whether that person is someone you see on the news, in your family photo, at your workplace, or in the mirror. But it must be received.

Look at Saul, the Hebrew of Hebrews, who became Paul, the apostle to the Gentiles; a blasphemer who became a believer, a predator who became a preacher, a terrorist who became a theologian, a law-keeper who became a grace-receiver, a scoundrel who became a saint. See and know that Jesus loves to put his mercy and grace on display in the lives of the worst of sinners.

Marvelous grace of our loving Lord,
Grace that exceeds our sin and our guilt!

Yonder on Calvary's mount outpoured,
There where the blood of the Lamb was spilled.

Grace, grace, God's grace,
Grace that will pardon and cleanse within;
Grace, grace, God's grace,
Grace that is greater than all our sin![28]

GROUP DISCUSSION GUIDE

Chapter 1: The Voice

1. When you picture a preacher telling people that they need to repent, what thoughts and feelings does that provoke in you? What do you think it provokes in non-Christians today?

2. Put yourself in the shoes of the Israelites who went out into the wilderness to hear John's message. Why might you be excited to hear it? Why might you be resistant to his message and his baptism?

3. The author told us to ask ourselves if we can identify the fruit of genuine repentance in our lives. Is there anyone who would give glory to God by sharing how God has worked in your life to generate the fruit of repentance? What evidence of turning away from sin is in your life? (No one will think you are bragging by answering this question, but someone will likely be encouraged by your answer.)

4. In Matthew 3:11, John said, "I baptize you with water for repentance, but he who is coming after me is mightier than I, whose sandals I am not worthy to carry. He will baptize you with the Holy Spirit and fire." What do you think John intended to communicate about the difference between his baptism and the baptism that Jesus would give to people?

5. What did John misunderstand from his study of the Old Testament scriptures? How did that prompt his question to Jesus from prison?

6. Do you think it is possible for a person to resist the conviction of the Holy Spirit so many times that they reach a point when they can no longer hear or respond to it? Why or why not?

7. What would it take for you to disrupt the status quo in your life so that you can live a life of repentance?

Chapter 2: The Family

1. What are some of the reasons Matthew may have chosen to begin his Gospel with a genealogy?

2. How can studying the genealogy of Jesus give us hope?

3. What evidence suggests that Joseph and Mary understood who Jesus was? What evidence suggests that they did not fully understand who Jesus was?

4. In order to become a member of Jesus's family, how much does a person have to understand about who Jesus is and why he came into the world?

5. Why do you think Jesus's siblings did not believe in him?

6. What did Jesus say makes a person family to him? What does that mean for how we relate to our biological family and our church family?

7. Is there someone in your family you are still hoping will put their faith in Christ? What hope does this chapter give you? How does this chapter challenge you?

Chapter 3: The Rock

1. What are some things that make true and lasting change difficult?

2. Why is it important to see that being transformed into the image of Christ begins with God taking the initiative rather than us making a decision?

3. If God must reveal himself to us for us to see who he really is, how does he do that? How can we position ourselves to receive that revelation?

4. What do you think Jesus meant when he said, "If anyone would come after me, let him deny himself and take up his cross and follow me"?

5. What are some of the ways that the Simon we see in the Gospels is very different from the Peter we see in Acts and 1 and 2 Peter?

6. If someone asked you how change happens in the life of a person who is joined to Christ, how would you answer?

7. Are there some specific changes you could make to your daily routine, your participation in the body of Christ, your prayer life, or the way you interact with the Bible that you think could result in some real change in your life?

Chapter 4: The Hypocrites

1. When you read the author's "You might be a religious hypocrite if . . ." statements, were there any you felt particularly convicted by (that you'd be willing to admit to the group)?

2. The people in Jesus's day admired the Pharisees for their strict adherence to the law, which they saw as righteousness. Are there people you admire for their righteousness? What is it about their lives that you see as admirable or righteous?

3. One fault of the Pharisees was that they ignored camel-sized commands while being overly concerned about lesser things. What are some ways we might have that same tendency today?

4. What are some warning signs that we, like the Pharisees, are more interested in silencing conviction than responding to conviction?

5. In the middle of the list of "woes," Jesus said, "The greatest among you shall be your servant. Whoever exalts himself will be humbled, and whoever humbles himself will be exalted" (Matt. 23:11–12). Is this an accepted truth in our culture? What kind of exaltation is Jesus talking about?

6. Jesus told Nicodemus that he had to be "born again." That phrase is often misunderstood or scorned in our day. What did Jesus mean by it? How does this new birth happen?

7. If the answer to hypocrisy is humility, can a person decide or try to be humble? If not, how does a person become humble? Is there anything you and I can do to foster genuine humility and authentic faith in our lives?

Chapter 5: The Crook

1. Go ahead and sing the song! You know you want to. As you consider this story as an adult, what stood out to you more than Zacchaeus's stature or his climbing a tree?

2. To get a sense of the disgust and hatred people had for tax collectors, perhaps we need to come up with some modern equivalents. Who are some specific people or categories of people that are hated today? Who are the people we might struggle to welcome if they showed up at our church seeking Jesus?

3. Throughout Luke we read numerous references to tax collectors and to rich people (Luke 5:27–32; 12:13–21; 15:1–2; 16:19–26; 18:18–

30). What pattern do you see? If we're familiar with that pattern in Luke's Gospel, how does it create a crisis or question in our minds when we read Luke 19:2?

4. The author mentioned several things that might have made Zacchaeus curious to see Jesus—the changes in the tax collectors who were baptized by John, Levi leaving everything to follow Jesus, the reputation Jesus had as someone who was friends with tax collectors, and the story Jesus told about a tax collector and a Pharisee. How do each of these interactions present a different aspect of the benefits of being joined to Jesus?

5. At the very beginning of the Bible, God sought after Adam and Eve when they were hiding, not up a tree but behind a tree. As the story of the Bible progresses, God sought out Abraham, who was not looking for him but was living in the land of Ur. In Romans 3, Paul quotes the Psalm that says, "No one seeks for God." What does this reveal to us about who was seeking whom in the story of Zacchaeus, or perhaps, what prompted Zacchaeus to seek Jesus? (Also see John 6:43–44; 15:16).

6. What do you think motivated Zacchaeus to announce that he would give away half of his goods to the poor and make fourfold restitution to those he had defrauded? What impact do you think that would have had in his community?

7. What are some ways Zacchaeus's business and personal life likely changed after Jesus's visit to his house? What were some implications of his announcement for his family? For the tax collectors who worked for him? For the believers in Jesus in Jericho?

8. Jesus made the statement, "Today salvation has come to this house" (Luke 19:9). When salvation came to Zacchaeus, and when it comes to any of us, there are various aspects to that salvation,

including election, calling, regeneration, conversion (faith and repentance), justification, adoption, sanctification, perseverance, and glorification. Spend some time seeking to define or describe these aspects of salvation. Which ones are evident in the story of Zacchaeus?

Chapter 6: The Opportunist

1. Judas was chosen by Jesus and witnessed all that the other disciples witnessed for three years. Yet Judas never came to genuine faith in Jesus. What does that reveal about Judas? About Jesus? About saving faith? What does it tell you about those who spend their whole lives involved in the church?

2. The author suggested that Judas's hardness of heart began with the breach of one commandment, "You shall not steal," a sin that he never confessed to Jesus. What specific impact does hidden, unconfessed sin have in our lives and in our relationship to Christ?

3. When you read about Mary's extravagant expression of love toward Jesus, how does it hit you? If you had been in the room at that dinner, do you think you would have seen it as worthwhile or as a waste? Why?

4. In what ways can you see yourself in Judas? In what ways can you see yourself in Mary?

5. The disciples around the table seemed open to examining the genuineness of their commitment to Jesus. Paul also calls for it in his second letter to the Corinthians, writing, "Examine yourselves, to see whether you are in the faith" (2 Cor. 13:5). How do we do that?

6. The author listed a number of scriptures that demonstrate that the shedding of Christ's innocent blood was not a waste. Is

there one that is either unclear to you or particularly meaningful to you?

7. What makes a life worthwhile? What makes it a waste?

Chapter 7: The Priest

1. In what way(s) was Israel's high priest "in the mercy business"?
   For what purpose did God establish the priesthood?

2. What does it mean that Caiaphas was the shadow and Jesus was
   the substance?

3. How had the role of high priest become dramatically different in
   Jesus's day from what God intended it to be?

4. What is the irony in Caiaphas's words, "It is better for you that one
   man should die for the people, not that the whole nation should
   perish" (John 11:50)?

5. Why was the death of Jesus the end of the priesthood, the end of
   the sacrificial system, and the end of the temple?

6. Why do you think some people never cry out to God for mercy?

7. Instead of coming to a corrupt priest like Caiaphas to confess our
   sins, we come to our Great High Priest, Jesus, to confess our sins.
   How does this change how we confess and what we expect?

Chapter 8: The Criminals

1. Why do you think it was important for Luke to emphasize the innocence of Jesus to his original readers? Why is it important to us
   as modern readers?

2. The story of Barabbas is one of the most vivid presentations of the
   principle of substitution in the Bible. What are some other ways

the Bible presents substitution, and why is it important? (Here are some references you may find helpful: Gen. 22:13; Lev. 16:21–22; Isa. 53:4–6; John 10:11; 2 Cor. 5:21; 1 Pet. 2:23–25.)

3. The crowd was willing for the penalty of taking innocent blood to fall on them and on their children. What was ironic about this in light of the promise given at Pentecost (Acts 2:39)?

4. What is the significance of the three different groups of people calling upon Jesus to save himself while he hung on the cross?

5. What do you hear in the words of the two thieves hanging beside Jesus that reveal what they believe about themselves and what they believe about the person being crucified between them?

6. How does the thief on the cross put an end to thinking that a Christian is someone who lives the Christian life well?

7. How could the promise Jesus gave to the thief, "Today you will be with me in paradise" (Luke 23:34), help you as you face your own death or the death of someone you love who is in Christ? What common fears about death does it relieve, and what common misconceptions about death does it refute?

Chapter 9: The Disciple

1. If we were going to design a trajectory or storyline for our lives, what do you think most of us would want it to look like?

2. Jesus told Cleopas and his companion that if they knew the Scriptures, they should have known that Jesus would suffer before being glorified. What are some ways they would have known? (Here are some verses that might help: Gen. 3:15; 37–50; Job; Ps. 22; Isa. 52:13–53:12.)

3. What feelings, words, or actions of ours demonstrate that we don't think our lives should include suffering if we are joined to Christ?

4. What were the two charges made against Stephen? How would you summarize his response to those charges?

5. Why was it likely not surprising to Stephen that they wanted to kill him? What might have comforted Stephen as he faced death?

6. How can Stephen's death provide comfort to us as believers in life and in death?

7. The author stated, "Confidence in the glory of the future enables us to endure the suffering of the present." What are some practical ways we can cultivate this confidence? How, specifically, does having confidence in future glory enable us to endure suffering?

Chapter 10: The Worst

1. Who might you add to the author's suggestions as "the last person" you think would become a Christian?

2. How did Saul's upbringing prepare him for his future ministry?

3. What made Paul think he was actually serving God in putting Christians to death?

4. Paul experienced something unique and supernatural on the road to Damascus that brought him to repentance and faith. How is our experience of coming to repentance and faith both similar and different from his?

5. If you were a believer in Paul's day, how would you have felt about welcoming him into your church? What do you think it was like for Paul to have relationships with believers he had persecuted? What would both sides have needed for those relationships to flourish?

6. Paul wrote, "Whatever gain I had, I counted as loss for the sake of Christ" (Phil. 3:7). What was it he previously saw as "gain" that he later counted as loss? What kinds of things might we think of as "gain," and then realize are "loss" when we consider them in the light of what helps us know Jesus as our Lord?

7. Why do you think Paul described himself as the "foremost" or "worst" of sinners (1 Tim. 1:15)?

8. How does the change that took place in Paul give you hope?

NOTES

1. Excerpted from full text of "The Power of Love," Bishop Michael Curry's Royal Wedding sermon, published by National Public Radio, May 20, 2018, https://www.npr.org/sections/thetwo-way/2018/05/20/612798691/bishop-michael-currys-royal-wedding-sermon-full-text-of-the-power-of-love/.
2. Douglas O'Donnell, *Matthew: All Authority in Heaven and on Earth* (Wheaton, IL: Crossway, 2013), 70.
3. Michael Horton, *Pilgrim Theology* (Grand Rapids, MI: Zondervan, 2011, 2012), 263.
4. Augustus Toplady, "Rock of Ages," 1763.
5. Julia H. Johnston, "Grace Greater Than Our Sin," 1910.
6. Johnston, "Grace Greater Than Our Sin."
7. I am indebted to F. B. Meyer for this imagery of Peter "letting down his nets" at Pentecost and later at the home of Cornelius, which is found in *Peter: Fisherman, Disciple, Apostle* (New York: Revell, 1920), 22.
8. Edward Mote, "The Solid Rock," 1843.
9. Jeff Foxworthy, "You Might Be a Redneck If . . ." Warner Brothers Records, Inc., 1993.
10. O'Donnell, *Matthew*, 687.
11. Joseph Hart, "Come, Ye Sinners Poor, and Needy," 1759.
12. John Newton, "Amazing Grace," 1772.
13. Wayne Stiles, "Sites and Insights: Jericho, City of Palms," *The Jerusalem Post*, October 18, 2012, https://www.jpost.com/Travel/Around-Israel/Sites-and-Insights-Jericho-city-of-palms/.
14. R. Kent Hughes, *Luke: That You May Know the Truth*, Preaching the Word (Wheaton, IL: Crossway, 2015), 656.
15. Sinclair Ferguson, "A Tale of Two Seekers" (sermon, First Presbyterian Church, Columbia, SC, Oct. 24, 2010).
16. James G. Small, "I've Found a Friend, O Such a Friend," 1866.
17. Isaac Watts, "When I Survey the Wondrous Cross," 1707.
18. Charitie Lees Bancroft, "Before the Throne of God Above," 1863.

19. Alexia Lafata, "#ItWasMe Is the Hashtag for Men Who Are Taking Responsibility for Rape Culture," *Elite Daily*, October 17, 2017, https://www.elitedaily.com/p/itwasme-is-the-hashtag-for-men-who-are-taking-responsibility-for-rape-culture-2930155/.
20. William Cowper, "There Is a Fountain Filled with Blood," 1772.
21. P. P. Bliss, "'Man of Sorrows,' What a Name," 1875.
22. Cowper, "There Is a Fountain Filled with Blood."
23. Cowper, "There Is a Fountain Filled with Blood."
24. Bliss, "'Man of Sorrows,' What a Name."
25. Charles Wesley, "O for a Thousand Tongues," 1739.
26. F. B. Meyer, *Saul: A Servant of Jesus Christ* (Fort Washington, PA: Christian Literature Crusade, 1983), 42.
27. Rosaria Butterfield, *The Secret Thoughts of an Unlikely Convert* (Pittsburgh, PA: Crown and Covenant, 2012), 63: "This was my conversion in a nutshell: I lost everything but the dog."
28. Johnston, "Grace Greater Than Our Sin."

BIBLIOGRAPHY

Batzig, Nick. "No Other Name." *He Reads Truth* (blog). June 9, 2016. Accessed January 10, 2019. http://hereadstruth.com/2016/06/09 /no-other-name/.

Beale, G. K. and Carson, D. A. *Commentary on the New Testament Use of the Old Testament*. Grand Rapids, MI: Baker Academic, 2007.

Begg, Alistair. "A Man Up a Tree." Sermon, Parkside Church, Chagrin Falls, OH. July 11, 2013.

Hoekema, Anthony A. *Saved by Grace*. Grand Rapids, MI: Eerdmans, 1989.

Lucas, Dick. "A Notable Cheat and a Notable Conversion." Sermon, St. Helens Bishopsgate, London. July 24, 2001.

Bruce, F. F. *Jesus: Lord & Savior*. Downers Grove, IL: InterVarsity Press, 1986.

Calvin, John. *Commentary on a Harmony of the Evangelists: Matthew, Mark, and Luke*. Grand Rapids, MI: Baker, 1989.

Carson, D. A. *The Gospel According to John*. The Pillar New Testament Commentary. Grand Rapids, MI: Eerdmans, 1991.

Ferguson, Sinclair. "A Tale of Two Seekers." Sermon, First Presbyterian Church, Columbia, SC. November 14, 2010.

Ferguson, Sinclair. "The Thieves Who Were Crucified with Him." Sermon, First Presbyterian Church, Columbia, SC, April 13, 2011.

Horton, Michael. *Pilgrim Theology*. Grand Rapids, MI: Zondervan, 2011, 2012.

Hughes, R. Kent. *Luke: That You May Know the Truth*. Preaching the Word. Wheaton, IL: Crossway, 2015.

Hughes, R. Kent. *Mark: Jesus Servant and Savior*. Preaching the Word. Wheaton, IL: Crossway, 2015.

Lockyer, Herbert. *All the Apostles of the Bible*. Grand Rapids, MI: Zondervan, 1972.

Metzger, Bruce. *The New Testament: Its Background, Growth, and Content*. Nashville, TN: Abingdon, 1983.

Meyer, F. B. *Paul: A Servant of Jesus Christ*. Fort Washington, PA: Christian Literature Crusade, 1983.

Meyer, F. B. *Peter: Fisherman, Disciple, Apostle*. New York, NY: Revell, 1920.

O'Donnell, Douglas. *Matthew: All Authority in Heaven and on Earth*, Preaching the Word. Wheaton, IL: Crossway, 2013.

Pink, Arthur W. *Exposition of the Gospel of John: Three Volumes Complete and Unabridged in One*. Grand Rapids, MI: Zondervan, 1945.

Reicke, Bo. *The New Testament Era: The World of the Bible from 500 B.C. to A.D. 100*. Philadelphia, PA: Fortress Press, 1968.

Ridderbos, Herman. *The Gospel of John: A Theological Commentary*. Grand Rapids, MI: Eerdmans, 1997.

Ryken, Philip Graham. *Luke Volume 1*. Reformed Expository Commentary. Phillipsburg, NJ: P&R, 2009.

Ryle, J. C. *Ryle's Expository Thoughts on the Gospels, Volume Two, Luke*. Grand Rapids, MI: Baker, 1977.

Segal, Marshall. "Let His Blood Be on Us." *DesiringGod.org* (blog). April 19, 2014. Accessed January 21, 2019. https://www.desiringgod.org/articles/let-his-blood-be-on-us/.

Skrine, Charlie. "Let Him Be Crucified." Sermon, St. Helen's Bishopsgate, London, England. March 4, 2018.

Smith, Colin S. *Heaven, How I Got Here: The Story of the Thief on the Cross*. Ross-Shire, Scotland: Christian Focus, 2015.

Smith, Colin S. *Heaven, So Near—So Far: The Story of Judas Iscariot*. Ross-Shire, Scotland: Christian Focus, 2017.

Thompson, Allan J. *The Acts of the Risen Lord Jesus: Luke's Account of God's Unfolding Plan*. Downers Grove, IL: InterVarsity Press, 2011.

Waters, Guy Prentiss. *The Life and Theology of Paul*. Orlando, FL: Reformation Trust, 2017.

Wright, Christopher. "Insults and Paradise." Sermon, All Souls Langham Place, London, England. March 25, 2007.

Wright, Christopher. "The One Who Searches Out the Lost." Sermon, All Souls Langham Place, London. July 20, 2008.

Yeulette, Paul. *Jesus & His Enemies*. Phillipsburg, PA: P&R, 2013.

GENERAL INDEX

Aaron, as the first high priest, 134–38

Abraham, 39, 40, 41, 45, 46, 53–54; shame of, 42

Adam, 154

Allen, Woody, 187

Ananias, 193, 194

Anas, 138

Andrew, 57, 59

baptism, 21, 22, 33; baptism of Jesus, 24–25; as a form of consecration, 24; by John the Baptist, 21, 23

Barabbas, 153–58, 164, 165

Bathsheba, 40, 42

Boaz, 41

Caiaphas, the last high priest, 133, 138–39, 175; plot of, 139; prophetic act of, 146–48; prophetic confusion of, 144–46; prophetic false testimony of, 143–44; prophetic words of, 139–43

change, in one's personal life, 55–57; real change begins with Jesus's call, 57–60; real change is granted by divine power, 67–71; real change requires divine revelation, 60–63; real change is tested by trials, 63–67

Christians, 187, 191, 199; early Christians, 183, 188; Jewish Christians, 172; modern Christians, 161

Cleopas, 168, 169

connectedness, to Christ, 74–75

Cornelius, 60

Curry, Michael, 13, 14

Cyrus the Great, 76

David, 39, 40, 41, 42, 45, 46; and the building of the temple, 176; shame of, 43; sons of, 138

Day of Atonement, 76, 148

death, Christian response to, 161–62

devotion, to Jesus, 120–21

disciples, the: abandonment of Jesus by, 162; confrontation over Jesus's intention to go to Jerusalem, 63–64; cowardly actions of at Jesus's arrest, 65; response to the question of who men think Jesus is, 61–62

discipleship, 170–71

Elijah, 17, 18, 19

Elizabeth, 17

SCRIPTURE INDEX

Also Available from Nancy Guthrie

Tracing 9 themes throughout the Bible, this book reveals how God's plan for the new heaven and the new earth, far better than restoration to Eden, is already having an impact in the world today.

For more information, visit **crossway.org**.

Seeing Jesus in the Old Testament Series

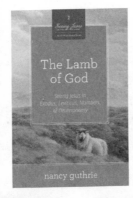

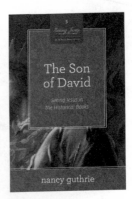

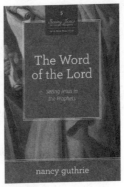

In these 10-week studies, Nancy Guthrie guides small groups to see the overarching theme of the work of Christ found in the Old Testament.

For more information, visit **crossway.org**.